Editor
Mary S. Jones, M.A.

Illustrator
Clint McKnight

Editor in Chief
Karen J. Goldfluss, M.S. Ed.

Cover Artist
Brenda DiAntonis

Art Coordinator
Renée Christine Yates

Imaging
Rosa C. See

Publisher

Mary D. Smith, M.S. Ed.

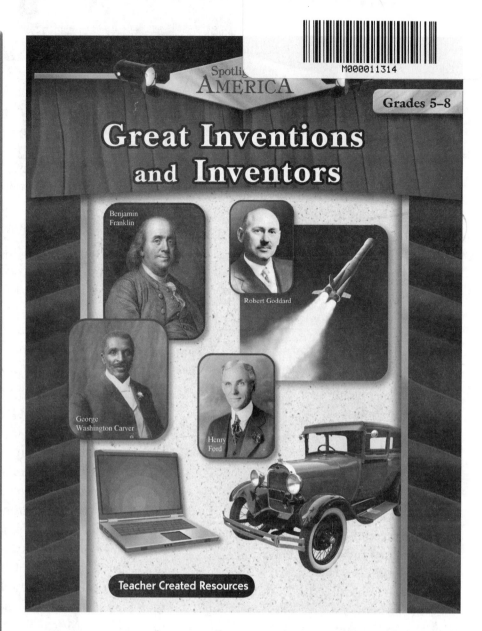

Grades 5–8

Spotlight AMERICA

Great Inventions and Inventors

Benjamin Franklin

Robert Goddard

George Washington Carver

Henry Ford

Teacher Created Resources

Author

Robert W. Smith

Teacher Created Resources, Inc.
6421 Industry Way
Westminster, CA 92683
www.teachercreated.com

ISBN: 978-1-4206-3234-7

© 2009 Teacher Created Resources, Inc.
Made in U.S.A.

Teacher Created Resources

Table of Contents

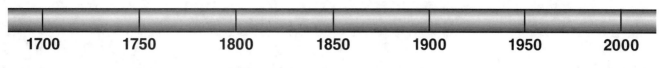

| 1700 | 1750 | 1800 | 1850 | 1900 | 1950 | 2000 |

Introduction

The *Spotlight on America* series is designed to introduce some of the seminal events in American history to students in the fifth through eighth grades. Reading in the content area is enriched with a balanced variety of activities in written language, literature, social studies, oral expression, and science. The series is designed to make history literally come alive in your classroom and take root in the minds of your students.

Inventive Forces

There were two driving movements in the development of the United States from a few struggling states hugging the eastern coast of North America to a nation that bestrode a continent and influenced all of the nations of the world. The westward movement of the American people across the continent was one force. The other force was a massive industrialization of the nation's economy. The inventive genius of the American people was the engine that drove this industrialization and connected the people scattered across a vast continent. The new United States government passed patent laws that protected the legal and financial rights of inventors and encouraged them to pursue their ideas with the hope that they would profit from their inventions.

Reading Comprehension

The reading selections and comprehension questions in this book serve to introduce some of the inventors who were vital to the success of the United States as a nation. Americans were a self-sufficient people from their earliest colonial days. They tinkered with different tools to enable them to farm better or work faster or reduce the amount of labor needed for a task. The 1800s saw a flood of life-changing inventions based often on new discoveries in electricity. The telegraph was invented by a professional artist who tinkered as a hobby. The telephone was invented by a teacher of the deaf who was trying to create a machine to help deaf people hear. The electric light bulb was invented by a man who spent his entire life improving existing inventions and inventing entirely new industries. At the first invention factory in the world, Edison filed more than a thousand patents in his lifetime.

Activities

The readings in this book set the stage for activities in other subject areas. The activities in social studies, written language, biography, and research are designed to help students recognize and empathize with the lives of these inventors. The science activities offer an opportunity for children to replicate some of the ideas and inventions of the past. Enjoy using this book with your students, and look for other books in this series.

| 1700 | 1750 | 1800 | 1850 | 1900 | 1950 | 2000 |

Teacher Lesson Plans for Reading Comprehension

Colonial Inventions and Inventors

Objective: Students will demonstrate fluency and comprehension in reading historically based text.

Materials: copies of Colonial Inventions and Inventors (pages 7–10) and Colonial Inventions and Inventors Quiz (page 36); additional reading selections from books, encyclopedias, and Internet sources for enrichment

Procedure

1. Reproduce and distribute the Colonial Inventions and Inventors reading selection listed above. Review pre-reading skills by briefly reviewing text and encouraging students to underline, make notes in the margins, write questions, and highlight unfamiliar words as they read.

2. Have students read the selection independently, in small groups, or together as a class.

3. As a class, discuss the following questions (or others of your choosing):
   - Who was the most interesting colonial inventor? Why?
   - Did the invention of the cotton gin have harmful or positive effects? Explain your position using facts from the reading.
   - Which was the most important invention for colonial Americans? Why?

Assessment: Have students complete the Colonial Inventions and Inventors Quiz and underline the sentences in the reading selection where the answers are found. Correct the quiz together.

19th-Century Inventions

Objective: Students will demonstrate fluency and comprehension in reading historically based text.

Materials: copies of 19th-Century Inventions: Power and Transportation (pages 11–12) and 19th-Century Inventions: Power and Transportation Quiz (page 37); copies of 19th-Century Inventions: The Communications Revolution (pages 13–17) and 19th-Century Inventions: The Communications Revolution Quiz (page 38); additional reading selections from books, encyclopedias, and Internet sources for enrichment

Procedure

1. Reproduce and distribute the 19th-Century Inventions reading selections listed above. Review pre-reading skills by briefly reviewing text and encouraging students to underline, make notes in the margins, write questions, and highlight unfamiliar words as they read.

2. Have students read the selections independently, in small groups, or together as a class.

3. As a class, discuss the following questions (or others of your choosing):
   - Why was the steamboat so important to people in the early 19th century?
   - Which inventor did you most admire? Why?
   - Which of the inventions you read about was the most important? Why?

Assessment: Have students complete the 19th-Century Invention Quizzes and underline the sentences in the reading selections where the answers are found. Correct the quizzes together.

Teacher Lesson Plans for Reading Comprehension *(cont.)*

Agricultural and Medical Inventions

Objective: Students will demonstrate fluency and comprehension in reading historically based text.

Materials: copies of Agricultural Inventions (pages 18–19) and Agricultural Inventions Quiz (page 39); copies of Medical Inventions (pages 20–24) and Medical Inventions Quiz (page 40); additional reading selections from books, encyclopedias, and Internet sources for enrichment

Procedure

1. Reproduce and distribute the Agricultural and Medical Inventions reading selections listed above. Review pre-reading skills by briefly reviewing text and encouraging students to underline, make notes in the margins, write questions, and highlight unfamiliar words as they read.

2. Have students read the selections independently, in small groups, or together as a class.

3. As a class, discuss the following questions (or others of your choosing):
   - Why was the mechanical combine so important to farmers and the country?
   - What did you most admire about George Washington Carver?
   - Which medical invention or discovery was the most important? Why?
   - Which medical inventions were especially important for children?

Assessment: Have students complete the Agricultural Inventions Quiz and the Medical Inventions Quiz and underline the sentences in the reading selections where the answers are found. Correct the quizzes together.

Cars, Planes, and Rockets

Objective: Students will demonstrate fluency and comprehension in reading historically based text.

Materials: copies of A Revolution in Speed: Cars, Planes, and Rockets (pages 25–29) and A Revolution in Speed: Cars, Planes, and Rockets Quiz (page 41); additional reading selections from books, encyclopedias, and Internet sources for enrichment

Procedure

1. Reproduce and distribute the Cars, Planes, and Rockets reading selection listed above. Review pre-reading skills by briefly reviewing text and encouraging students to underline, make notes in the margins, write questions, and highlight unfamiliar words as they read.

2. Have students read the selection independently, in small groups, or together as a class.

3. As a class, discuss the following questions (or others of your choosing):
   - Which inventor would you have rather worked with: Henry Ford, the Wright brothers, or Robert Goddard? Explain your choice.
   - Which invention—the automobile, the plane, or the rocket—was the most important? Why?
   - What kind of invention in transportation is needed today? Explain your idea.

Assessment: Have students complete the A Revolution in Speed Quiz and underline the sentences in the reading selection where the answers are found. Correct the quiz together.

Teacher Lesson Plans
for Reading Comprehension *(cont.)*

The Computer Revolution

Objective: Students will demonstrate fluency and comprehension in reading historically based text.

Materials: copies of The Computer Revolution (pages 30–31) and The Computer Revolution Quiz (page 42); additional reading selections from books, encyclopedias, and Internet sources for enrichment

Procedure

1. Reproduce and distribute The Computer Revolution reading selection listed above. Review pre-reading skills by briefly reviewing text and encouraging students to underline, make notes in the margins, write questions, and highlight unfamiliar words as they read.

2. Have students read the selection independently, in small groups, or together as a class.

3. As a class, discuss the following questions (or others of your choosing):

   • Why are computers so important in modern life?

   • Which computer innovation is most important to you?

   • What do you expect computers to be able to do in the future?

Assessment: Have students complete The Computer Revolution Quiz and underline the sentences in the reading selection where the answers are found. Correct the quiz together.

Common Inventions

Objective: Students will demonstrate fluency and comprehension in reading historically based text.

Materials: copies of Common Inventions (pages 32–35) and Common Inventions Quiz (page 43); additional reading selections from books, encyclopedias, and Internet sources for enrichment

Procedure

1. Reproduce and distribute the Common Inventions reading selection listed above. Review pre-reading skills by briefly reviewing text and encouraging students to underline, make notes in the margins, write questions, and highlight unfamiliar words as they read.

2. Have students read the selection independently, in small groups, or together as a class.

3. As a class, discuss the following questions (or others of your choosing):

   • Which was the most useful invention mentioned in the selection?

   • Which problem in ordinary life today needs to be solved by an invention?

   • Which of the inventions mentioned in the selection would you least want to be without?

Assessment: Have students complete the Common Inventions Quiz and underline the sentences in the reading selection where the answers are found. Correct the quiz together.

 Reading Passages

Colonial Inventions and Inventors

Becoming an Inventive People

The people who settled the American colonies in the 1600s and 1700s were primarily immigrants from Europe. Most were farmers who hoped to make a better life for themselves in the New World. They brought with them the tools and farming methods used in England and on the European continent. However, they soon learned that in this new world, they faced challenges and opportunities they hadn't encountered in Europe. The soil was different, as were the weather and growing seasons.

Their experiences were different, too. Some of the new immigrants learned to adjust their methods by learning from the Native Americans. Squanto was a Wampanoag Indian who taught the Pilgrim settlers how to plant corn with groups of seeds in mounds spread about in the rocky New England soil. He showed them how to bury a fish with the seeds to provide fertilizer for the growing plants. Farmers found that European plow models worked poorly in most colonial soils. Settlers kept trying to find ways to improve their farming methods and tools. They also developed better ways to store food, adopted some Indian foods for their gardens, and learned to adapt to different weather patterns.

Jefferson's plow

Thomas Jefferson

Thomas Jefferson is most famous today because he helped invent a nation, the United States, and became the third president of the country. He also had a very inventive and creative mind. He was particularly interested in improving farming. He experimented with several different plow designs that would work better in turning over the tough sod and heavy soils in the colonies. He invented a better design for the moldboard of the plow, the curved part of the plow that turns over the soil. Jefferson's plow was easier for a horse or an ox to pull, and it became popular with farmers.

Jefferson also experimented with many seeds for grains like oats and wheat, finding those that grew best in American soils. He is even credited with popularizing tomatoes as a food.

Reading Passages

Colonial Inventions and Inventors *(cont.)*

Jefferson's Inventions

Jefferson's creativity extended into many areas. He invented codes that could be used for sending secret messages. He was a diplomat in Europe and wanted to communicate with his colleagues in America without letting the authorities in France and England know America's plans. He wrote so many letters that he invented a device that copied his letters as he wrote them. Jefferson taught himself architecture and built one of the most remarkable homes in America at Monticello on his Virginia plantation. The house had many unique and practical features, as well as a classical design. He invented a dumbwaiter in the house. This was an elevator to carry food from the storage area in the basement to the upper parts of the house. He also invented a swivel chair so that he could move easily around his desk.

Benjamin Franklin

Ben Franklin is probably the best-known inventor of the colonial and revolutionary era. His experiments with electricity demonstrated the practical side of his nature and that of American inventors in general. His kite experiment, by which he proved that lightning is a form of electricity, is well known. His practical mind led from this discovery to the lightning rod, an invention that deflected the power of a lightning strike harmlessly into the ground. This invention saved countless numbers of homes and barns from fire, the most serious danger to property in most colonial settlements.

Franklin tried to use electricity in many ways. He even tried to electrocute a turkey but ended up shocking his audience instead. His Franklin stove was a great improvement over fireplaces because it kept heat within a contained area and also improved cooking times. He invented bifocal glasses because he was having trouble seeing as he became older. He studied weather patterns, the direction of thunderstorms, the flow of the Gulf Stream current, methods for fighting fire, and built convenient versions of chairs and ladders. Ben Franklin was the perfect example of the inventive American spirit.

 Reading Passages

Colonial Inventions and Inventors *(cont.)*

Benjamin Banneker

Benjamin Banneker was the grandchild of a white indentured servant (who earned her freedom after seven years) and a black slave she bought and freed. Banneker was born in 1731 in Maryland, a free man of color who grew up on a farm owned by his African-American parents. His father adapted techniques of irrigation he remembered from Africa. The channels and dams he dug made his farm very productive and helped neighbors learn effective methods of irrigation. Banneker had an opportunity to attend school and was very good in math. As he grew older he designed clocks, studied astronomy, and learned to survey land. He published an almanac in the 1790s and worked as a surveyor who helped design the new city of Washington, D.C.

Sybilla Masters

Sybilla Masters was typical of many of the women and men of the colonial and revolutionary era. She knew from personal experience that grinding up corn into flour to be used to make cornmeal was a long and tiring job. In 1712, Masters invented a machine that used hammers to do the job. It was quicker and did a better job. She wanted to get a patent on her invention. A patent is a legal document that guarantees that the inventor gets credit for the invention and has to be paid an agreed-upon amount of money by anyone who wants to produce products using the patented idea. However, women were not allowed to get patents at that time, so she went to England and got the patent in her husband's name. Later, Masters invented a new kind of fabric for hats using palmetto leaves.

David Rittenhouse

David Rittenhouse was a very successful colonial surveyor who made his own instruments and compasses. Surveying land was an important and valuable skill in the American colonies. Benjamin Banneker learned to survey, and so did George Washington, who used the skill to map lands on the western frontier when he was a British officer fighting the French before the American Revolution. Rittenhouse also designed and made the first telescope in America. It was so well made that he was able to discover that Venus had an atmosphere surrounding the planet. Rittenhouse also designed and made clocks and was a friend and associate of Benjamin Franklin.

 Reading Passages

Colonial Inventions and Inventors *(cont.)*

Improving Inventions

Many colonial inventors didn't get credit or money for their inventions. For example, Pennsylvania wagon makers gradually improved wagons for farmers, and western settlers developed the Conestoga wagon, which became the most popular vehicle for traveling through the western frontier. Gunsmiths made rifles by hand, and many gunsmiths made improvements that allowed rifles to fire faster and at greater distances. Many American soldiers brought their own weapons when they joined the revolutionary army of George Washington, and some had more effective weapons than did British soldiers.

Eli Whitney

Eli Whitney invented the cotton gin, a simple instrument that revolutionized the cotton industry because it separated cotton fibers from the seeds 50 times faster than could be done by hand. It was patented on March 14, 1794. Wire spikes pulled cotton through slots too narrow for the seeds. The cotton gin was so simple that people didn't buy the product from Whitney. Instead, they made their own gins, and so he made very little for his invention. This invention also made cotton growing very profitable, which led to an even greater use of slaves.

cotton gin

When war threatened to break out between the new United States and France in the late 1790s, Whitney convinced the War Department to buy thousands of rifles from him because he had invented a system for producing guns that were exactly alike and so had interchangeable parts. Each worker assembled only a small part of the rifle. Labor costs were cheaper. This was the beginning of the factory system, which would make goods cheaper but also lead to lower wages and a less-skilled labor force.

Setting the Stage

The creative and innovative inventors of the colonial and revolutionary era in the 1600s and 1700s provided the attitude of innovation and creativity that would develop in the next two centuries into a whole new world of inventions for factories, farms, and homes. It would revolutionize the worlds of business, medicine, science, transportation, and communication; and utterly change the quality of life for everyone.

Reading Passages

19th-Century Inventions: Power and Transportation

Inventing the Industrial Revolution

The Industrial Revolution built up steam in the United States from about 1790 to 1860. The United States had a rapid rise in factory growth, and many machines were designed, invented, or improved to speed up work within the factory. Constant improvements were made in railroad locomotives and equipment. National roads through the eastern wilderness were begun, canals were dug between natural waterways, and wagons were improved. Sources of power drove industry and encouraged invention. Steam power, electricity, and oil became major forces influencing inventors.

Robert Fulton and the Steamboat

The greatest invention of the early 1800s was the steamboat. Early inventors of this craft were unsuccessful because people were fearful of the look of the boats and expected the engines to explode. Robert Fulton's invention changed that. He built the *Clermont* according to his own design 1807. After a demonstration trip up the Hudson River, Fulton began full-time service in September 1807 between New York and Albany, a distance of 150 miles. Fulton and his wealthy partner, Robert Livingston, built other boats, including in 1811 the *New Orleans*, the first steamboat to travel the 2,000-mile journey down the Ohio and Mississippi Rivers to New Orleans. This invention completely transformed business and transportation in the Mississippi River Valley and allowed goods and people to travel down the river and back up in what was then the fastest mode of travel.

Fulton's Career

Like many other American inventors, Robert Fulton showed his talent at an early age. As a child, he created household tools for his mother and skyrockets for a community celebration. He designed a paddlewheel for a rowboat and a rifle of his own. In his late teens, he became a successful painter of portraits and miniatures. After a few years studying painting in Europe with American artist Benjamin West, he became interested in science and engineering. He designed new types of canal boats and locks. Fulton invented machines to make ropes, cut marble, and spin flax. He designed and built one of the earliest submarines, which worked but did not have enough power under water to succeed as a warship. Later in his life he designed torpedoes, a harpoon gun, and steam warships. Fulton died of pneumonia at the age of 49.

Reading Passages

19th-Century Inventions: Power and Transportation *(cont.)*

Edwin Drake Invents an Industry

Sometimes an inventor doesn't just create a machine or a process, but an entire industry. In 1857, Edwin Drake was an ex-railroad construction worker who invested his savings in a small Pennsylvania business that gathered oil to be sold for making medicine from seeps where the oil leaked onto the surface through cracks in the rocks.

Drake decided to drill for the oil the way some companies drilled for salt in shallow water. He invested in saltwater safe drilling equipment, designed a derrick to sit over the oil seep, and bought a steam engine to power the drill. He also bought two other farms where oil was seeping out.

Drake's first efforts were total failures. The drill bits broke. The salt mining crew he hired didn't know how to drill in the rocky Pennsylvania soil, and the machinery kept breaking. Drake fired the crew and went back to step one. He studied drilling techniques. He designed and built a drilling machine that worked like a steam hammer, pounding into the rocky soil. He hired a blacksmith to forge tougher drill bits.

In July 1859, Drake hired a new crew and began drilling again through a hard rock ledge and finally into dirt below it. The team worked into August, getting as deep as about 65 feet. One morning in late August, Drake found a pool of oil around his derrick. He had found a way to reach underground oil.

Drake went on to drill more wells and to supply a steady flow of oil to customers by carrying barrels of it in wagon trains to customers. The oils that were wanted by industry and homeowners were kerosene (used for lighting and stoves), tar, and thick lubricating oils. Gasoline was actually separated and burned off because there was no use for it.

The oil industry quickly developed as rich investors bought fields and created even more effective drilling methods. Oil became one of the primary factors in the development of American industry and, eventually, transportation. With the development of the automobile and aircraft, gasoline would, of course, become a very important oil product.

Reading Passages

19th-Century Inventions: The Communications Revolution

The Age of Electricity

Three American inventors and many lesser-known mechanics and tinkerers would change the lives of people throughout the world and totally transform human communications for all time. They would use the latest advances in electricity to create the telegraph, the telephone, and the electrically powered home and factory. These advances in electricity would then spur the extraordinary inventions of the 20th and 21st centuries in aircraft, radio, television, computer technology, lasers, and other complex machines for communication and transportation.

Samuel Morse

Samuel Morse was one of eleven children. His father was a preacher and writer. Morse was a fair student at the academy he attended and an average student at Yale University. He spent most of his time drawing and painting. Eventually, he went to England where he studied with Benjamin West, a famous American artist. Morse was an impatient art student and often distracted by other interests. He returned to America and achieved some success as a painter. After a second trip to Europe, he became interested in the new science of electricity and magnetism. He wanted to invent a machine to send messages over a long distance, an idea other people were also working on.

Supported by friends at New York University where he taught art, Morse designed his own telegraph. He also created the Morse code to make messages clear and simple. Samuel Morse was granted a patent for his design in 1837. In March 1843, Morse was able to convince Congress to grant him $30,000 to build an experimental telegraph line from Washington, D.C. to Baltimore, Maryland, 35 miles away. In March 1844, Morse sent the message, "What hath God wrought!" along the line, and his invention became immediately popular. He was paid by developers for the rights to his patent, and telegraph lines soon sprung up across the country. It became the most important communication tool of its time. Many other inventors would make improvements on the process for more than 50 years.

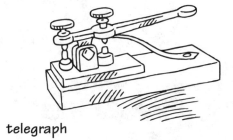
telegraph

19th-Century Inventions: The Communications Revolution *(cont.)*

Joseph Henry

Joseph Henry was an American physicist and Princeton College professor whose work in electromagnetism was essential to the development of many of the great communications breakthroughs. He developed strong horseshoe magnets essential to the development of Morse's telegraph and provided Morse with a lot of technical help, for which Morse did not give him credit.

Henry designed the battery-powered booster relays, insulation for the wire, and glass insulators for the telegraph poles. Henry became the head of the Smithsonian Institution, the leading agency for invention and scientific development in the nation. All inventors using electricity and electromagnetism owed a debt to Henry's scientific investigations. He, in turn, owed a great deal to the discoveries of the English scientist Michael Faraday.

Alexander Graham Bell

Alexander Graham Bell was born on March 3, 1847 in Edinburgh, Scotland. His father taught students how to speak correctly.

His mother, a painter, was deaf. Young Alex grew up with two brothers. Before starting school at 10 years old, Bell read many books, studied nature, and became interested in his father's work and how sound is created. Alex and his brothers even made a talking doll that said, "Mama."

Bell left school at age 14 and soon became a speech teacher like his father. He became very interested in the scientific advances made in electricity and built a telegraph to use in experiments. After his brothers died from tuberculosis, his parents and Bell left Scotland to live in Canada. Bell got a job in the United States as a teacher of the deaf in Boston. He experimented with a harmonic telegraph, which he hoped would help deaf people hear. He was able to send sounds and eventually words as he refined his invention. In 1876, a few days after his 29th birthday, Alexander Graham Bell sent a message to his assistant, Thomas Watson, in another room. It said, "Mr. Watson, come here. I want you."

Reading Passages

19th-Century Inventions: The Communications Revolution *(cont.)*

The Telephone

Bell filed for a patent a few hours before another inventor, Elisha Gray, filed a patent on a similar device. Bell eventually won the legal battles to the rights for his invention. In 1876, Bell demonstrated his device at a Centennial Exposition in Philadelphia and to important world leaders like Queen Victoria. The telephone soon became a success in the business world and with homeowners. About 130,000 phones were already in use just five years after the invention.

Bell, Thomas Edison, and other inventors continued to refine and improve the telephone. Bell went on to invent the graphophone, an improvement of Edison's phonograph, and to work on other inventions, including ones related to his continuing interest in helping deaf people hear. He married one of his students, Mable Hubbard, whose father had helped Bell with funds for his telephone. Bell helped arrange for Anne Sullivan to help Helen Keller, a child who was deaf, blind, and unable to speak.

Bell's Other Inventions

Bell invented many other devices, including the tetrahedral kite and models of hydrofoil boats, which traveled rapidly over the top of the water. He was even part of a team of inventors who were asked to save President Garfield's life. The president had been shot, and Bell was asked to develop a device for finding the bullet embedded in the president's abdomen. They were not successful, and the president died of his wounds, but the probe he invented would later save many soldiers' lives.

Thomas Alva Edison

Thomas Edison was considered the greatest inventive genius of his time. In a period when hundreds of men were working on every kind of improvement for the machinery that was driving the nation's industry, Edison was unique because his inventive interests covered so many industries and because they totally changed American life. No other inventor has worked on so many different inventions or so profoundly affected the modern world.

Reading Passages

19th-Century Inventions: The Communications Revolution *(cont.)*

Edison's Youth

In a sense, Samuel Morse's invention of the telegraph started Edison's career. Edison had been a curious and unusual student who, like most teens of his generation, left school by the eighth grade and went to work. He sold newspapers and small items on the railroad routes near his hometown in Michigan. He even published his own newspaper and had a science lab in a baggage car until one of the chemicals started a fire and the lab was banned. Edison became interested in becoming a telegrapher, a popular and well-paying job for young men. He saved the son of a telegrapher from being run over by a train, and out of gratitude the father taught him how to work the telegraph.

Edison used those lessons to get a telegrapher's job on the train and soon began trying to improve the machine. His first patent was for a vote recorder, which used some of the telegraph machinery. It didn't sell, but his other improvements led to the stock-ticker; the quadruplex telegraph, which could send four messages at once; and many other refinements and improvements of telegraph equipment.

In 1876 at the age of 29, Thomas Edison opened the first invention factory in the world at Menlo Park, New Jersey. He assembled a team of scientists, engineers, machinists, and other skilled men who worked on improvements to the telegraph and the newly-invented telephone. It was here that he invented the phonograph while trying to improve the telephone. He boasted that he would invent a functioning incandescent light bulb in six weeks. Despite his boast, it took him almost a year before he and his team found a truly successful filament (carbonized thread and bamboo) for the first successful light bulbs.

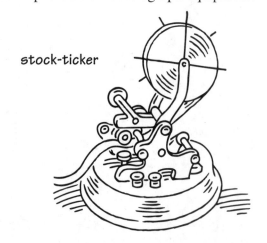

stock-ticker

phonograph

Reading Passages

19th-Century Inventions: The Communications Revolution *(cont.)*

Edison's Vision

Edison's extraordinary vision is especially evident in these efforts because he set out to invent the entire industry of electric power to be provided to businesses and homes. He created an electric generator, an electric motor, and in 1882, opened a power plant in New York City that eventually became the model for providing electric power to the nation and the industrialized world.

In the years that followed, Edison's teams worked on improving the phonograph, inventing primitive motion-picture equipment, removing valuable metals from ore, creating an effective cement, and designing an electric motor and an electric starter for cars.

Edison worked with many businessmen and investors over the course of his career, and he was often involved in lawsuits over patent rights on certain inventions. He was a close friend of the car manufacturer Henry Ford and was widely respected in the business community for the extraordinary drive that his inventions provided in the development of new products.

Nikola Tesla

Nikola Tesla was a Serbian immigrant to the United States who had remarkable insights into the nature of electricity. He went to work for Edison in 1884. Within months they had begun a feud that lasted a lifetime. Edison had a strong personal and financial commitment to the concept of direct current, a system in which electric current flows in one direction from a source to its use. Tesla envisioned a system called alternating current, in which

the flow of electric current switches back and forth many times each second. He invented a motor using this AC current, which was much more efficient than the DC-current motors in use then.

When Edison refused to consider his invention, Tesla sold his idea to another major industrialist, George Westinghouse. The extraordinary power and efficiency of the new system led to its rapid acceptance. Tesla designed nearly 700 other pieces of electrical equipment, and AC current is used almost exclusively today. Tesla and Edison would have received the 1912 Nobel Prize in Physics for their work in electricity but their personal animosity was so great that they wouldn't do even that together and the prize went to someone else.

Agricultural Inventions

Cyrus McCormick — Mechanical Combine

Cyrus McCormick's father tried to invent a combination harvester for most of the 1820s and finally gave up. His 19-year-old son, Cyrus, studied the harvesting techniques of the farmers in the Shenandoah Valley of Virginia where they lived. His observations led to the creation of his first combine. He mounted a paddle wheel on a platform above a knife with metal blades to cut the grain. He built a platform behind the cutting apparatus to hold the stalks of grain. He then mounted a second set of paddles above a rotating drum on the platform. The paddles beat the cut grain so the seeds would fall off into a storage bin below. The straw would be raked and baled on the same machine.

It took many attempts for McCormick to coordinate the actions of each of these separate components. His original model was eight feet wide and drawn by two horses. The various movements of the equipment were coordinated with drive belts and timed by the speed of the wheels of the machine as it moved through the fields. This original

combine was able to harvest wheat and oats as fast as a team of 30 men harvesting in a field. The McCormick harvesters were an instant success and Cyrus kept improving his designs. By 1870, he was selling combines pulled by 40 horses and cutting 35-foot-wide swaths through the field. The development of this extraordinary machine led to the invention of other specialized agricultural machines. In 1837, a blacksmith named John Deere invented the steel plow, which made plowing much easier and more effective. Farm tractors were developed soon after the automobile. Seed planters and hay rakes were improved over time. The invention of barbed wire protected farmers' crops from wandering cattle.

George Washington Carver

George Washington Carver began life as a slave on the farm of Moses Carver and his wife near the town of Diamond in Missouri. Bandits kidnapped his mother and George when he was still an infant. His mother was never found, but George, a sickly child, was returned. When the American Civil War ended, slavery was outlawed, but the Carvers treated George and his older brother almost like sons.

Reading Passages

Agricultural Inventions *(cont.)*

The Plant Doctor

George was a very bright child who quickly learned how to grow plants, to read, and to paint. As a young boy, he was known in his community as "the plant doctor" and raised his own secret garden with many kinds of plants. When he became a teenager, George spent several years traveling across the Midwest trying to get an education. He even tried to homestead a farm in Kansas for a time. He finally was accepted by Simpson College and later studied at Iowa State College. He improved his artistic skills and became an expert in the study of hybrid plants and the best agricultural practices.

In 1896, Carver accepted a position with Booker T. Washington at Tuskegee Institute in Alabama, a college devoted to offering African-Americans a chance to improve their lives. He taught agricultural science, botany, biology, ran an experimental farm, and helped students see the relationships between all of the skills they were learning.

Carver used the lab he developed to create many inventions related to plants. He developed a faster-growing cotton plant able to resist the boll weevil, which destroyed cotton. He taught farmers to rotate crops and improve their land by planting black-eyed peas to return nutrients to the soil. He developed more than 40 recipes for using these peas. George became the father of chemurgy, the science of finding new uses for products such as sweet potatoes, peas, peanuts, and even acorns. George invented more than 300 uses for peanuts, including cheese, cream, oils, shampoo, ink, flour, face powder, soap, medicine, and vinegar. He invented about 160 uses for sweet potatoes, including coconut, molasses, dye, shoe polish, flour, glue, vinegar, ink, and a kind of rubber.

Carver was offered a very large salary and a lab to use by Thomas Edison. Instead, George decided to remain at Tuskegee as a teacher trying to improve life for all Southern farmers, black and white. He did not file for patents beacause he regarded his inventions as belonging to all mankind. Carver was honored for his inventions in his last years as Americans recognized his enormous contributions to agriculture and to the Southern farmers he served.

Reading Passages

Medical Inventions

As in all fields, inventions in medicine have occurred in many nations and cultures. Here are a few of the important American contributions.

Anesthesia

One of the major causes of death in the medical treatments of the 1700s and 1800s was the terrible pain involved in treatment. Amputations during war, childbirth, care of badly burned patients, and many other medical treatments were made worse by the extreme shock and excruciating pain. In 1845, Charles Jackson, an American chemist, discovered that ether was an effective anesthetic. William Morton, an American doctor, saw ether being used as a party drug and decided to use it for reducing tooth pain in his patients. To administer the drug, he used a sealed jar containing ether-soaked sponges with an air valve hooked to a long rubber tube. This was connected to a rubber mouthpiece. Dr. Morton's efforts were successful, but ether was unpleasant smelling and irritated the lungs. Chloroform soon replaced ether as an anesthetic, especially in childbirth.

Braces for Teeth

In 1880, an American dentist named Norman W. Kingsley invented braces and the science of orthodontics, which means "straight teeth." The first braces were ugly and uncomfortable. They had heavy metal plates anchored to teeth with dental cement and connected by thick wires. J.N. Farrar invented the first modern braces, and the first school for teaching orthodontics was founded in the early 1900s.

Hearing Aids

Alexander Graham Bell was working on a device to help deaf children hear when he invented the telephone. Miller Reese Hutchinson used many of Bell's ideas and invented the first electric hearing aid in 1901. He called it the Telephone Transmitter. It had a microphone to catch sound and turn it into an electric signal. An amplifier made the signal stronger, and an earpiece turned the signal back into sound. However, it was bulky and hard to use. By 1935, hearing aides were small enough to wear. Today, hearing aids are small enough to wear behind or in the ear.

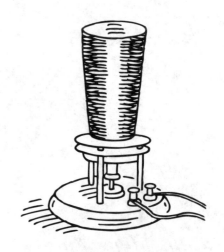

Reading
Passages

Medical Inventions (cont.)

Polio and the Iron Lung

One of the most feared diseases of the first half of the 20th century was polio. Polio was called infantile paralysis because it primarily attacked children and destroyed or paralyzed their nervous systems. It was caused by a virus and killed thousands of children. Many others were permanently crippled. Polio was spread by contaminated food and water and could make a victim suffocate and die within hours. It was essential to have a breathing device that could keep a child alive for a few days or weeks until some of the effects of the virus wore off and the child could breathe again.

In 1926, a physician named Philip Drinker took an idea from his brother, who was studying how animals breathe. He designed a box large enough to hold a human and used a modified vacuum cleaner to pump air in and out of it. Pumping the air out of the box caused the patient's chest to rise and air was pulled into the lungs. When air was pumped in, the chest fell, and air was removed from the lungs. Dr. Drinker's first patient was an eight-year-old girl who was near death. She regained consciousness in minutes. By 1931, a commercial version of his iron lung was being sold to hospitals all over the world. Today a ventilator and facemask help patients to breathe.

Curing Polio

In 1950 alone, more than 30,000 new cases of polio infected American children. Two research doctors using different approaches were determined to find a cure for polio. Dr. Jonas Salk was funded by research funds from the government and private sources. In 1952, Salk experimented with a "killed virus" which he tested first on monkeys and then with children who had been infected with polio and children who had never been infected. By 1954, after many more trials, Dr. Salk declared that his vaccine worked, and children were vaccinated across the country. Working on the suggestion of microbiologist Dr. Albert Sabin, Salk developed a "live virus" vaccine, which was too weak to cause polio but was strong enough to cause permanent immunity to the disease. By 1961, polio had decreased in the United States by 95 percent. Today, because of these two medical inventions, new cases of polio have virtually disappeared.

Reading
Passages

Medical Inventions *(cont.)*

Genetic Engineering

Humans have about 30,000 genes, and the health of a person is very closely connected to these genes. Each gene located in the cells has a complex set of chemical instructions made up of a substance called DNA. Genes direct how the body builds itself and how it acts. They decide an individual's height, hair and eye color, and even a person's susceptibility to diseases like cancer.

In 1953, American scientist James Watson and Englishman Francis Crick discovered the double-helix structure of DNA. This discovery allowed scientists to invent ways to change genes in living things. This genetic engineering will have an enormous impact on medicine in the future. Two American biochemists, Stanley Cohen and Herbert Boyer, became pioneers in this field when they were able to cut a strand of microscopic bacteria and insert a gene from another living organism into it.

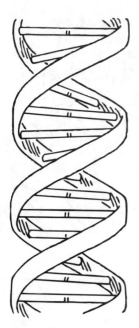

This was the first in a series of successful efforts to invent new or improved types of plants and animals that can be used to treat many illnesses. For example, a type of bacteria that produces insulin has been engineered to help diabetics stay alive. Another has produced human growth hormone. Bacteria genes have been introduced into plants to make them insect-resistant.

By the year 2000, scientists had mapped the entire human genome, the sequence of every gene in the human body. This will have far-reaching effects on disease detection and cures. Gene therapy, the introduction of genes into the body to cure specific illnesses, is already being researched with such diseases as cystic fibrosis, hemophilia, and immune deficiency.

Another side-product of these genetic discoveries is DNA fingerprinting. Each individual has a unique pattern of DNA sequences. Scientific detectives can determine if blood, hair, or tissue from a crime scene matches the DNA of a suspect. It is also used to identify the remains of a person and to determine family relationships among animals.

Reading Passages

Medical Inventions *(cont.)*

MRI Scanner

X-rays and CAT scans are good at seeing bones in the human body. But with these, the soft tissue is difficult to see. In 1977, an American, Raymond Damadian, led a team of researchers who built the Magnetic Resonance Imaging scanner. The first scanner Davidian's team built was able to detect a tumor in a cancer patient. The team then built a full-sized scanner that used very strong magnets to create radio signals in the body. The scanner then detects these signals and converts them into an image on a television screen.

An MRI scanner can see bones, but it also shows soft tissue like the brain or body tissue inside bones. MRIs are not as effective with the heart or lungs because movement in these organs blurs the images. Not moving is critical to the success of an MRI image, so patients are required to be immobile for up to 60 minutes while they are in the tube where the images are being taken. The loud, distracting noise of the scanner can also bother patients.

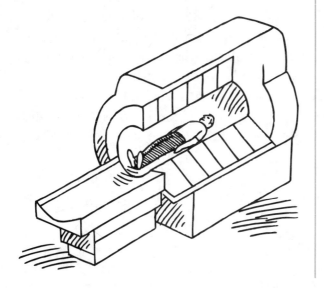

Nystatin

Bacteria and viruses are well known as potential agents of disease. Fungi also cause many diseases and deaths. Fungi are plants, but they do not have chlorophyll and do not produce their own food. They include mushrooms and molds among the more than quarter-million kinds of fungi. They can cause such skin diseases as ringworm. In 1948, Dr. Elizabeth Hazen and Dr. Rachel Brown began a determined search for cures to fungal diseases. They grew 50 small dishes of each of 300 kinds of mold, which the researches believed might be sources of disease. They tested these 15,000 dishes of fungi with 30 different kinds of potential antibiotics suggested by scientists, botanists, and Native American healers.

The doctors eventually tested over 200 potential antibiotics on more than 25,000 types of fungi. They found that one group of bacteria, the streptomycetes, killed almost every kind of fungi. The two scientists isolated the specific bacteria in the streptomycete, which killed the fungi, and in 1950 created the first extremely effective antifungal medicine, Nystatin, which has saved countless lives. In the years from 1948 to its introduction in 1950, the two doctors did over 3 million individual tests and grew 1.5 million dishes of fungi during 60,000 hours.

 Reading Passages

Medical Inventions *(cont.)*

Chemotherapy

In 1933, a 15-year-old girl watched her grandmother wither away and die of stomach cancer. There were no effective treatments for cancer, but Gertrude Elion was determined to change that. By 1937, she had graduated with honors from Hunters College, but she couldn't get a good job because of the Great Depression and because of her gender. She worked part-time jobs and got her Master's degree from New York University by taking night and weekend courses. During World War II, she got a job at the Burroughs Wellcome research labs working with DNA and trying to develop new drugs.

After five years of research, Elion uncovered a chemical process essential to cell growth that is changed in cancerous cells. Within six months of this discovery, Elion invented two anticancer drugs called Thioguanine and 6-MP. The drug named 6-MP, working with other medications, cured childhood leukemia in 80 percent of the children who received it. This was the first effective anticancer treatment for any form of cancer.

In 1957, Elion discovered that a form of the same anticancer drug, 6-MP, called Imuran, could suppress the body's immune system long enough to allow organ transplants. Transplants never worked before the use of this drug. The chemical compounds Gertrude Elion created attacked cancer cells and left normal cells unaffected. Millions of people have been saved by her inventions and others that followed, based on her work.

Arthroscopic Surgery (Endoscope)

Basil Hirschowitz, a Belgium-born doctor, became a teacher and researcher at the University of Michigan. He wanted to find a way to see inside joints and body organs during surgery. He and a graduate student named Larry Curtiss experimented with a number of materials. They tried glass rods, different types of glass fibers, and finally a transparent fiber made from silicon dioxide, which was less fragile than glass and would not break inside the patient. They discovered that long, flexible fibers of silicon dioxide carried light and worked perfectly. The first successful use of the endoscope was to see inside the joint during a knee operation in 1957. The doctors needed to open only an inch-long incision for the scope to enter the body and illuminate the area. Within 20 years, the endoscope was being used in all kinds of arthroscopic surgeries to see inside joints, body organs, and blood vessels.

endoscope

Reading Passages

A Revolution in Speed: Cars, Planes, and Rockets

The 20th century saw revolutionary developments in the ability of humanity to move across vast expanses at great speed. The car, the airplane, and the rocket changed many aspects of modern life.

Henry Ford

Henry Ford didn't invent the automobile, he invented a way of life. Ford was born on a farm in 1863 in what is now Dearborn, Michigan. He didn't like farm chores, but he loved to tinker with anything mechanical. He fixed farm machinery and took apart clocks. He left home when he was 16 and built freight cars and repaired machines. He returned to the farm for a while, married, and in 1891 went to Detroit where he worked for the Edison Company.

Ford had a shop where he worked on a self-propelled vehicle, which he completed in 1896. There was one problem: the vehicle was too large to get out the door, and Ford had to use an ax to widen the door so he could get it out. He called his vehicle the *quadricycle*. It had a motor, could travel in two speeds, and was steered by a tiller (like a boat).

After several setbacks, Henry formed the Ford Motor Company in 1903. He wanted to build inexpensive cars that ordinary people could afford, rather than a few vehicles for the very wealthy.

The Model T — "Tin Lizzie"

In 1908, Henry Ford developed a design called the Model T. Ford decided that it would be the only model of car they would make. Every car would be exactly alike, and was available in only one color—black. The car originally cost $825, much less than other cars being made at the time. The car was built high off the ground to keep from getting stuck in ruts and mud. His company sold 10,000 cars the first year.

 Reading Passages

A Revolution in Speed: Cars, Planes, and Rockets *(cont.)*

The Assembly Line

The greatest of Ford's inventive ideas was to apply the idea of the moving assembly line to car manufacturing. The system went into place in 1913. The cars moved along a line from one station to the next, where each worker attached one piece to each car rather than building a car entirely alone. Ford made sure that at each stop there was time to do just one operation so the line would not be held up.

Different Ideas

The assembly-line system sped up production enormously. By 1916, Ford's company was able to make 700,000 "Tin Lizzies," as they were called, and he was able to reduce the price to $360. Ford was able to reduce the time it took to make one Model T from 6 hours to 90 minutes. Ford also had several other ideas that were truly different for his time. In 1914, workers got paid about $2.50 a day for a 10-hour day. He decided to pay his workers $5 a day for an 8-hour shift. It increased productivity because workers were anxious to keep their jobs. Their pay allowed them to make enough money to purchase the cars they were making. It also made buying Ford cars popular with other working Americans.

Ford also developed the idea of Ford franchises, which he sold throughout the country. These sales and repair shops used Ford products, sold cars, and repaired vehicles. The franchises increased his profits and control over the entire system. Henry also bought supply companies and materials so that he would not be held up by shortages, fluctuations in prices, or poor quality.

For a time, Henry Ford dominated the automobile industry in the country. However, he was soon challenged by other automakers, who adopted most of his innovations and brought their own ideas to the marketplace. Many inventors created popular improvements to the automobile. Mary Anderson, for example, invented windshield wipers, and Paul Gavin developed a practical car radio in 1929.

Model T

 Reading Passages

A Revolution in Speed: Cars, Planes, and Rockets *(cont.)*

The Wright Brothers

The airplane changed the world every bit as much as the automobile. Many inventors had been trying to create a heavier-than-air powered machine. The Wright brothers were mechanically minded tinkers, much like Henry Ford and Thomas Edison. Their single-minded commitment to flight paid off on a windy day at Kitty Hawk, South Carolina, in December 1903.

Early Life

Wilbur Wright was born on an Indiana farm on August 19, 1867. Orville was born exactly four years later. Their mother encouraged the boys in working on their many mechanical contraptions. When they grew up, the brothers started their own bicycle company, through which they sold and repaired the popular new bicycle models. They also designed and built their own bicycles. The boys learned to use all types of tools and became skilled metalworkers and woodcrafters. They became very interested in gliders and the possibility of powered flight.

Wilbur Wright

Orville Wright

Building a Plane

The Wrights took up bird watching and started experimenting. They were trying to solve three major questions, which they felt were at the heart of manned flight: What was the best wing design for lifting the flying machine? How could they control the machine in the air? What could they use that was sufficiently strong to power the machine through the air?

"Wing-warping"

The brothers built a double-decker box kite-shaped glider. They devised a system of cords attached to the corners of their double-wing glider. The cords could be controlled so that the wings could be twisted down at one end or the other as needed for variations in wind and air pressure. They called this process "wing-warping." The patent they eventually took on this system is still the basis of the moveable flaps, called *ailerons*, used in modern aircraft. They tested the glider at Kitty Hawk, South Carolina, and continually made improvements over several years.

Building the Flyer

The brothers built their plane model based on their glider. They made and tested dozens of propeller designs and found that propellers could provide both lift into the air and forward thrust. They decided to use two propellers rotating in opposite directions for stability. They also decided to design and construct their own motor to use on the plane.

Reading Passages

A Revolution in Speed: Cars, Planes, and Rockets *(cont.)*

The First Manned Flight

The Wrights went to Kitty Hawk and assembled their plane. On December 17, 1903, after failing earlier in the week, the brothers put their *Flyer* on a monorail track along a sand dune. With the help of local lifeguards, they pushed the plane down the rail and into history. Orville made the first flight, which went 120 feet in 12 seconds. The fourth flight went 852 feet and lasted 59 seconds. They became the first to fly a heavier-than-air powered airplane. The plane was smashed by wind before a fifth flight.

Later Improvements

Although the brothers informed the press of their success and even had photographs, it would be almost five years before the Wrights received credit for their accomplishment. They spent years improving their aircraft and trying to interest the United States government and foreign nations in their flying machines. The Wrights eventually became the acknowledged leaders of the aviation world for a few years, until Wilbur died in 1912 and Orville sold their plane company in 1915.

Other Aviation Innovators

Samuel Langley, an American physicist and astronomer with government funding, had been competing with the Wright brothers and nearly beat them, but his plane crashed into the Potomac River earlier in the year.

In 1907, Alexander Graham Bell formed the Aerial Experiment Association to advance aviation. He contributed the idea of a three-wheel undercarriage for landings and take-offs and ailerons for stability and maneuverability. The same year, Glenn Curtiss began to design and manufacture planes. In the years to come, many inventors would create even more effective and larger aircraft.

 Reading Passages

A Revolution in Speed: Cars, Planes, and Rockets *(cont.)*

The Rocket

Robert Goddard's invention of the liquid-fueled rocket in 1926 is the key discovery that makes space travel and exploration possible. Early types of rockets using gunpowder and solid fuel couldn't attain enough height to escape the pull of Earth's gravity. Wernher von Braun would help his adopted country reach for the stars.

Robert Goddard

Robert Goddard was born in the small city of Worcester, Massachusetts, in 1882. As a child, the science-fiction writing of Jules Verne and H.G. Wells inspired him. He became fascinated with the idea of rockets. Goddard received his physics degree and continued his interest in rockets. He soon found that the chemicals and powders he was using wouldn't get his rockets into space. He needed a large amount of fast-burning explosives to get a rocket out of Earth's atmosphere. In 1913, Goddard filed two patents for rockets based on his research. One was for a multi-stage rocket, and the other was for using two tanks filled with combustible materials, such as gasoline and liquefied nitrous oxide, which would mix and supply power to a rocket. In 1917, Goddard received a $5,000 grant from the Smithsonian Institution and later a U.S. Army grant for $20,000 to continue his work. He developed a motor that ran by forcing gasoline into a fuel chamber with compressed oxygen.

He also invented the bazooka, a rocket-like weapon.

On March 16, 1926, Goddard succeeded in the first liquid-fueled rocket flight on his aunt's farm near Auburn, Massachusetts. The flight lasted only two-and-a-half seconds and rose only 41 feet. Two years later he launched a rocket that went twice as high. During a long career as a rocket scientist, Goddard filed over 200 patents and made many technical advances. During World War II, he discovered that the Germans had studied his work and used it to convert his Nell rockets (named for his wife) into the V-2 rockets that the Germans used to bomb London. Robert Goddard died in 1945.

Wernher von Braun

Wernher von Braun designed and built rockets in Germany during World War II. At the end of the war, he arranged to surrender himself and his team of rocket experts to the Americans. They were relocated to Huntsville, Alabama, where they designed rockets for the United States. The early Saturn and Jupiter rockets von Braun designed were created to carry Americans into space. His Juno and Redstone rockets carried communications satellites into space and were the backbone of America's intercontinental ballistic missile program.

 Reading Passages

The Computer Revolution

Computers have radically changed many facets of American life. Although they have been influenced by many inventions and innovations throughout the world, many of the crucial ones have been created in the United States.

First Steps

The Mark I is generally considered to be the first digital computer. Dr. Howard Aiken, a Harvard professor, began work on the machine in 1937. He was aided in his work by Thomas Watson, the founder of IBM. The machine was given to the navy in 1943. The Mark I was 51 feet long, 8 feet high, and 5 feet deep. It used 3,300 mechanical relays to process information and had a four-horsepower motor. It was used for calculating firing angles on naval guns, computing shock waves from atomic bomb blasts, and other military problems. It could do calculations in one day that previously took six months, although it was very slow by today's standards. Dr. Grace Hopper, a navy lieutenant, was a programmer on the Mark I. Later she worked on the ENIAC and UNIVAC computers. She invented computer languages that allowed computers to communicate with each other.

Technological Advances

John Bardeen, Walter Brattain, and William Shockley, who worked for Bell Labs, invented the transistor in 1947. They were working with elements called semi-conductors. These have areas that conduct electricity in very different ways. Transistors are essential to many electronic devices, including the computer.

Silicon chips, which hold integrated circuits, were built in 1958 and 1959 by Jack Kilby and Robert Noyce. The microprocessor, which places all of a computer's circuits on a single silicon chip, was invented in 1969 by Ted Hoff. It shrank the central processor cabinet of a computer to the size of a small file cabinet.

Space War, the first video game, was created by Stephen Russell and several friends at the Massachusetts Institute of Technology in 1962. It was a part of the program for the DEC PDP-1 which then cost over $120,000. The computer mouse was invented in 1965 by Doug Englebart. His original name for the device was "X–Y Position Indicator for a Display System."

Reading Passages

The Computer Revolution *(cont.)*

Personal Computers

The first small personal computer was the Altair 8000, released in 1975. Bill Gates wrote its operating system as his first programming job, but the computer could only respond with a few LED lights.

Steve Wozniak designed the first true personal computer, the Apple I, in 1976. He connected a control board he designed to a TV monitor, a power supply, a keyboard, and transformers and enclosed it all in a plastic case. Some Apple Is sold, but they didn't quite catch on. He and his partner, Steve Jobs, introduced the Apple II computer in 1977. It was more powerful, easy to use, and had good color graphics. Sales of the Apple II took off, and the personal computer revolution was born.

Apple II

Supercomputer

Seymour Cray created the first supercomputer in 1976. It had 200,000 integrated circuits and was able to perform 150 million operations in a second. Its successor, the Cray 2 supercomputer, could perform 1,600 million operations in a second.

Internet

The Internet was created in the United States in 1963 when a network of computers was hooked up to protect military information in the event of a nuclear attack. It was called the ARPAnet. The first communication between computers in different places happened in October 1969, when data was sent from one California university computer to another.

The Internet became an international network in the 1980s, and the World Wide Web in the 1990s made the Internet available to all. It allows the exchange of text within seconds around the world. One of the innovations stemming from this web is email, created in 1971 by Ray Tomlinson. The first message was a string of letters from the top of the keyboard. Telnet, invented in 1972, could control a computer from a distance. FTP (file transfer protocol) was developed in 1973.

The compact disc (CD) was jointly invented by two companies, Philips and Sony, in 1983. CDs can store sounds, written words, music, and movies. An American company called Xybernaut invented wearable computers in 2002. They are called Poma ("portable multimedia appliances").

Reading
Passages

Common Inventions

Americans have been skilled in creating useful small tools and inventions that have made life easier at home and in business. Some of these inventions affect our lives every day.

Common Needs and Uncommon Thinkers

Earle Dickson had an accident-prone wife. She was always getting cuts and burns. He worked for Johnson & Johnson, a company that made bandages for hospitals. He cut the bandages into small pieces, added adhesive tape and a covering, thereby inventing Band-Aids® in 1920 to make her life and many other lives easier.

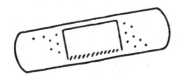

Many inventors were common people with one special idea for improving life. Abraham Lincoln had an idea for getting ships across shallow water from one deep lake or river to another. He designed a machine for moving a ship across shallow water. He built a model and filed a patent, but the device was never built. He is the only president to hold a patent. (Thomas Jefferson did not patent his inventions. He wanted everyone to share his ideas.)

Walter Hunt owed $400 to the draftsman who drew illustrations for his inventions. Hunt agreed to give the draftsman the rights to any invention he could make in three hours with a piece of bent wire. In one afternoon in 1849, he invented the modern safety pin, and the draftsman was more than well paid.

Hunt also invented a forerunner of the repeating rifle and a sewing machine, but he didn't patent it because he was afraid it would put too many people out of work.

In the 1830s, John Howe, a New York City doctor, invented a machine for making straight pins for clothes and attaching papers. The machine produced 72,000 pins per day, although it took 60 people to stick the pins into packages for sale.

Toothpaste has existed since Roman times, but in 1892 Dr. Washington Sheffield put it in a tube. Whitcomb Judson invented the zipper in 1893. It wasn't very successful. Gideon Sundback improved it in 1913, and his version is still being used for several items. Marvin Stone invented the drinking straw in 1888. In 1873, Levi Strauss and Jacob Davis invented a new kind of pants using rivets, small metal shafts, to hold the pockets in place, even if they were full of tools. Levi's became very popular with miners and other workingmen.

 Reading Passages

Common Inventions *(cont.)*

African-American Inventors

Elijah McCoy was the son of slaves who escaped to Canada. In 1872, he was working on an American railroad and realized that stopping the train to lubricate pistons, gears, and bearings cost time and money. He developed an invention that would automatically lubricate the train while it was moving. He became so famous for the skill with which he made his equipment that his name became a symbol for quality, "the real McCoy." He filed over 50 patents for inventions, including a lawn sprinkler and a type of tire.

Granville T. Woods had more than 50 patents. He invented a railroad telegraph to allow conductors to send and receive messages on a moving train.

Lewis Latimer was a designer and draftsman. He was an expert in the lighting industry and helped Alexander Graham Bell draft the plans for his telephone patent. He helped build the first electric plants in Philadelphia, Montreal, and New York City.

In the early 1900s, Madame C.J. Walker was a freed slave who did laundry for a living. She had trouble with her own hair, so she developed compounds that straightened and smoothed hair for African-American women. She started her own business by selling her products door to door. They soon became very popular, and Mrs. Walker became one of the wealthiest women in America.

 Reading Passages

Common Inventions *(cont.)*

Women Inventors

Stephanie Kwolek invented Kevlar, a tough plastic material used in tires, bulletproof vests, and space vehicles, in 1966. It is one of 28 different patents held by this DuPont company chemist who specializes in synthetic fibers, those made by man from chemicals.

Fannie Farmer invented the modern-day cookbook in 1896. It was the first cookbook to use precise, standardized measurements. Not only did it sell incredibly well, but it led to a major development in publishing. Thousands of cookbooks are in print today, and all use the standardized terms that Farmer invented.

Other Women Inventors

There were many other women inventors. Beulah Henry had 49 patents for common, household inventions, including a snap-on umbrella. Martha Coston developed signal flares used by the Union Navy during the Civil War. Sarah Mather invented both a lamp and a telescope for submarines. Ruth Handler invented the Barbie Doll and special products for women who had surgery. Josephine Cochran invented the first dishwasher in 1886 with a wooden tub, a wire basket, and a hand pump.

Hedy Lamarr, a movie actress, escaped from Austria at the beginning of World War II. In the United States, she and a friend invented a system for guiding torpedoes by radio signals. Anna Corey Baldwin invented a milking machine for cows. Margaret Knight received her first of more than 20 patents in 1870 for a machine that cuts, folds, and pastes paper bags—creating the first successful square-bottomed paper shopping bags.

Reading
Passages

Common Inventions *(cont.)*

Products We Wouldn't Want to Do Without

Charles Goodyear worked for years trying to make rubber that could remain pliable in any kind of weather. In 1939, he accidentally dropped a mixture of rubber and sulfur on the stove. He tested it in the cold and found that it worked. He called the process *vulcanization,* and rubber became useful in many different machines, tools, and products, such as tires.

In 1953, Columbia University physicist Charles Townes invented the maser using microwave radiation. In 1960, Theodore Maiman, a young Stanford graduate, used visible light instead of microwave radiation and developed the laser that can be used for everything from cutting steel to eye surgery. But it was Albert Einstein who first proposed the idea for the laser.

In a trip to the Arctic, Clarence Birdseye watched Eskimos freeze fish on the ice. He discovered that this fast method of freezing did no damage to the flesh of the fish and left it tasting almost the same as fresh fish. He went home and did some experiments with different kinds of freezing devices and invented the frozen-food business.

Elisha Otis invented the safety elevator in 1853. Almon Strowger was a teacher and undertaker who invented the telephone exchange in 1891 so that a caller could dial a number without a telephone operator. Will Kellogg invented the breakfast cereal, Corn Flakes®, in the early 1900s. Percy Spencer invented the microwave oven in the 1940s. In 1946, Edwin Land produced the Polaroid® instant camera.

Colonial Inventions and Inventors Quiz

Directions: Read pages 7–10 about colonial inventions and inventors. Answer these questions based on the information in the selection. Circle the correct answer in each question below. Underline the sentences in the reading selection where the answers are found.

1. Who taught the Pilgrim settlers how to plant corn and other seeds in the rocky New England soil?
   a. Thomas Jefferson
   b. Squanto
   c. Benjamin Franklin
   d. Eli Whitney

2. Which future president improved the plow?
   a. Benjamin Franklin
   b. Benjamin Banneker
   c. George Washington
   d. Thomas Jefferson

3. Who designed and built the first telescope made in America?
   a. David Rittenhouse
   b. Sybilla Masters
   c. Benjamin Franklin
   d. Thomas Jefferson

4. What did Sybilla Masters invent?
   a. a corn grinder
   b. a telescope
   c. a fabric for making hats
   d. both a and c

5. Which African-American helped survey the new city of Washington, D.C.?
   a. Thomas Jefferson
   b. Benjamin Banneker
   c. Sybilla Masters
   d. George Washington Carver

6. Which planet's atmosphere did David Rittenhouse study?
   a. Venus
   b. Earth
   c. Jupiter
   d. Mercury

7. Which of these inventions did Benjamin Franklin not create?
   a. bifocal glasses
   b. lightning rod
   c. improved chairs and ladders
   d. plow

8. Which of these inventions did Thomas Jefferson create?
   a. a letter copier
   b. a dumbwaiter
   c. a swivel chair
   d. all of the above

9. Who studied the Gulf Stream current and thunderstorms?
   a. Benjamin Banneker
   b. Benjamin Franklin
   c. Thomas Jefferson
   d. Eli Whitney

10. Who invented a system for making guns with interchangeable parts?
    a. Eli Whitney
    b. Benjamin Franklin
    c. David Rittenhouse
    d. Squanto

19th-Century Inventions: Power and Transportation Quiz

Directions: Read pages 11–12 about 19th-century inventions in the areas of power and transportation. Answer these questions based on the information in the selection. Circle the correct answer in each question below. Underline the sentences in the reading selection where the answers are found.

1. When did the Industrial Revolution develop in the United States?

   a. between 1790 and 1860

   b. after 1860

   c. from 1690 to 1760

   d. between 1900 and 1950

2. What inventions did Robert Fulton make as a child?

   a. paddlewheel for a rowboat

   b. a steamboat

   c. a rifle

   d. both a and c

3. Who was Benjamin West?

   a. an inventor

   b. president of the United States

   c. an artist

   d. an oil driller

4. In what year did Edwin Drake succeed in drilling for oil?

   a. 1869

   b. 1859

   c. 1857

   d. 1807

5. Which of these ships was invented by Robert Fulton?

   a. *Clermont*

   b. *New Orleans*

   c. *Constitution*

   d. both a and b

6. Which oil product was burned up when oil was drilled because it did not have any use?

   a. kerosene   c. gasoline

   b. lubricating oil   d. tar

7. Which group of miners was a model for Edwin Drake when he decided to drill for oil?

   a. salt miners

   b. coal miners

   c. gold miners

   d. iron-ore miners

8. Which invention completely transformed business and transportation in the Mississippi River Valley?

   a. flatboat   c. steamboat

   b. railroad   d. canal

9. For which of the following was oil not used in the 1860s?

   a. medicine

   b. lubricating machines

   c. lighting

   d. automobiles

10. Which of the following machines did Robert Fulton invent?

    a. torpedoes

    b. a harpoon gun

    c. machines to make rope

    d. all of the above

19th-Century Inventions:
The Communications Revolution Quiz

Directions: Read pages 13–17 about 19th-century communications inventions. Answer these questions based on the information in the selection. Circle the correct answer in each question below. Underline the sentences in the reading selection where the answers are found.

1. Which of these inventions was created by Nikola Tesla?
   a. alternating current
   b. direct current
   c. the telegraph
   d. the phonograph

2. Who sent the message, "What hath God wrought!" over the line from Washington, D.C. to Baltimore?
   a. Samuel Morse
   b. Thomas Edison
   c. Alexander Graham Bell
   d. Joseph Henry

3. Which physicist helped Samuel Morse invent the telegraph but did not receive credit for the help?
   a. Joseph Henry
   b. Nikola Tesla
   c. Thomas Edison
   d. Benjamin West

4. Which of these inventions was not invented by Alexander Graham Bell?
   a. tetrahedral kite
   b. incandescent light bulb
   c. telephone
   d. graphophone

5. Who created the first invention factory at Menlo Park, New Jersey?
   a. Alexander Graham Bell
   b. Samuel Morse
   c. Thomas Edison
   d. Joseph Henry

6. What did Edison use carbonized thread and bamboo for?
   a. telephone lines
   b. phonograph
   c. stock-ticker
   d. incandescent light bulb

7. What did Edison invent while trying to improve the telephone?
   a. an electric motor
   b. phonograph
   c. cement
   d. electric car starter

8. Whose science investigations with electricity and electromagnets led to the telegraph, telephone, and many other communications inventions?
   a. Joseph Henry
   b. Thomas Watson
   c. Thomas Edison
   d. Alexander Graham Bell

9. Which president's life did Alexander Graham Bell try to save?
   a. Abraham Lincoln
   b. James Garfield
   c. Theodore Roosevelt
   d. John F. Kennedy

10. In 1876, what message did Alexander Graham Bell send to his assistant with the harmonic telegraph?
    a. "Mr. Watson, come here. I want you."
    b. "Mr. Watson, I want you in here."
    c. "Mr. Watson, come here please."
    d. "Mr. Watson, come here. You're needed."

Agricultural Inventions Quiz

Directions: Read pages 18–19 about agricultural inventions. Answer these questions based on the information in the selection. Circle the correct answer in each question below. Underline the sentences in the reading selection where the answers are found.

1. What farming tool did John Deere invent in 1837?

   a. mechanical combine

   b. steel plow

   c. barbed wire

   d. all of the above

2. Who invented the first mechanical combine?

   a. Cyrus McCormick

   b. George Washington Carver

   c. John Deere

   d. Thomas Edison

3. Which of the following products was not invented by George Washington Carver from peanuts?

   a. face powder

   b. shampoo

   c. shoe polish

   d. vinegar

4. What is the name of the science of finding new uses for products?

   a. chemistry

   b. botany

   c. chemurgy

   d. biology

5. Which of these products did George Washington Carver find new uses for?

   a. peanuts

   b. sweet potatoes

   c. peas

   d. all of the above

6. Which of the following offered George Washington Carver a very large salary and a lab to use?

   a. Booker T. Washington

   b. Thomas Edison

   c. Moses Carver

   d. Simpson College

7. How old was Cyrus McCormick when he started work on the mechanical combine?

   a. 67

   b. 19

   c. 40

   d. 31

8. In what year did McCormick sell a combine, which was pulled by 40 horses and cut a swath 35 feet wide?

   a. 1870

   b. 1837

   c. 1831

   d. 1902

9. Who was known as "the plant doctor" when he was growing up?

   a. Moses Carver

   b. Cyrus McCormick

   c. John Deere

   d. George Washington Carver

10. Where did George Washington Carver teach from 1896 until his death?

    a. Tuskagee Institute

    b. Simpson College

    c. Iowa State College

    d. Harvard University

Medical Inventions Quiz

Directions: Read pages 20–24 about medical inventions. Answer these questions based on the information in the selection. Circle the correct answer in each question below. Underline the sentences in the reading selection where the answers are found.

1. What did Miller Reese Hutchinson invent in 1901?

   a. MRI scanner

   b. electric hearing aid

   c. endoscope

   d. anesthesia

2. Which word means "straight teeth"?

   a. braces

   b. anesthesia

   c. chemotherapy

   d. orthodontics

3. Which scientist discovered a vaccine that nearly eliminated polio?

   a. William Morton

   b. Jonas Salk

   c. James Watson

   d. Gertrude Elion

4. What medical discovery allows doctors to see inside joints and body organs during surgery?

   a. iron lung

   b. endoscope

   c. MRI scanner

   d. genetic engineering

5. What American scientist worked with Francis Crick to discover the double helix structure of DNA?

   a. James Watson

   b. Gertrude Elion

   c. Philip Drinker

   d. Norman W. Kingsley

6. For which condition was the iron lung used to help children breathe?

   a. asthma

   b. toothache

   c. polio

   d. measles

7. Which of these medications is used to treat diseases caused by fungi?

   a. ether

   b. Nystatin

   c. chemotherapy

   d. chloroform

8. Which doctor used ether as an anesthetic to reduce tooth pain?

   a. William Morton

   b. Norman Kingsley

   c. Albert Sabin

   d. Philip Drinker

9. What disease are the drugs developed by Gertrude Elion used to treat?

   a. polio

   b. cancer

   c. ringworm

   d. diabetes

10. What is the name for the complete sequence of every gene in the human body?

    a. DNA

    b. human genome

    c. double helix

    d. hormone

A Revolution in Speed: Cars, Planes, and Rockets Quiz

Directions: Read pages 25–29 about automobile, airplane, and rocket inventions. Answer these questions based on the information in the selection. Circle the correct answer in each question below. Underline the sentences in the reading selection where the answers are found.

1. What was the "Tin Lizzie"?
   a. a girl
   b. the first airplane
   c. an early rocket
   d. the Model T car

2. Who applied the idea of the moving assembly line to the production of cars?
   a. Thomas Edison
   b. Henry Ford
   c. Robert Goddard
   d. Orville Wright

3. What was the name for the system of cords used by the Wright brothers to adjust to variations in wind and air pressure?
   a. rudder
   b. rear wing
   c. wing-warping
   d. pulleys

4. Which man was not involved in early efforts to build and improve planes?
   a. Samuel Langley
   b. Robert Goddard
   c. Glenn Curtiss
   d. Alexander Graham Bell

5. How long was the fourth flight of the Wright brothers on December 17, 1903?
   a. 3 miles in 3 minutes
   b. 120 feet in 12 seconds
   c. 852 feet in 59 seconds
   d. 41 feet in 3 seconds

6. When was the first successful launch of a liquid-fueled rocket made?
   a. 1926
   b. 1945
   c. 1903
   d. 1913

7. What problem did Henry Ford have with the quadricycle he designed?
   a. it went too fast
   b. it was too big for the door
   c. it was too high
   d. it was too heavy

8. How much money did Ford decide to pay his workers for an eight-hour shift in 1914?
   a. $2.50 in total
   b. $5.00 an hour
   c. $2.50 an hour
   d. $5.00 in total

9. Which of these rockets was designed by Wernher von Braun?
   a. Saturn
   b. Jupiter
   c. Juno
   d. all of the above

10. Who did Robert Goddard name his rockets after?
    a. H.G. Wells
    b. presidents of the U.S.
    c. his wife, Nell
    d. Wilbur Wright

The Computer Revolution Quiz

Directions: Read pages 30–31 about computer-related inventions. Answer these questions based on the information in the selection. Circle the correct answer in each question below. Underline the sentences in the reading selection where the answers are found.

1. Which of the following men invented the microprocessor?

   a. Ted Hoff
   b. Jack Kilby
   c. Howard Aiken
   d. John Bardeen

2. What was the Mark I computer used for?

   a. to play video games
   b. to calculate firing angles
   c. to control planes
   d. to study the brain

3. What is another name for the "X–Y Position Indicator"?

   a. video game
   b. mouse
   c. transistor
   d. silicon chip

4. What did Seymour Cray invent?

   a. computer mouse
   b. supercomputer
   c. transistor
   d. compact disc

5. Who invented the first true personal computer?

   a. Bill Gates
   b. Steve Wozniak
   c. Ray Tomlinson
   d. Seymour Cray

6. What computer could perform 1,600 million operations in a second?

   a. Apple I
   b. Mark I
   c. Cray 2
   d. Apple II

7. Who invented the transistor?

   a. William Shockley
   b. John Bardeen
   c. Walter Brattain
   d. all of the above

8. What did Grace Hopper help invent?

   a. Mark I computer
   b. computer languages
   c. silicon chip
   d. computer games

9. What did Ray Tomlinson invent?

   a. CD
   b. email
   c. Internet
   d. World Wide Web

10. Which of these inventions is a portable wearable computer?

    a. Telnet
    b. Xybernaut
    c. Poma
    d. ARPAnet

Common Inventions Quiz

Directions: Read pages 32–35 about common inventions. Answer these questions based on the information in the selection. Circle the correct answer in each question below. Underline the sentences in the reading selection where the answers are found.

1. Which of these people invented the safety pin?

    a. Earle Dickson

    b. Walter Hunt

    c. Washington Sheffield

    d. Whitcomb Judson

2. What product did Charles Goodyear invent?

    a. vulcanized rubber

    b. safety elevator

    c. Corn Flakes®

    d. Kevlar

3. What native activity did Charles Birdseye observe that gave him an idea for his invention?

    a. cows being milked

    b. Eskimos freezing fish

    c. boats in shallow water

    d. cooking meat

4. Who created better pants for workingmen?

    a. Levi Strauss

    b. Jacob Davis

    c. Will Kellogg

    d. both a and b

5. What invention was created to help an accident-prone wife and other people with small cuts and wounds?

    a. zipper

    b. Band-Aid®

    c. laser

    d. paper bag

6. What does "the real McCoy" stand for?

    a. a medicine

    b. quality

    c. a hair straightener

    d. a kind of chocolates

7. Which African-American inventor had more than 50 patents, including a railroad telegraph?

    a. Elijah McCoy

    b. Lewis Latimer

    c. Garrett Morgan

    d. Granville T. Woods

8. Which American president is the only one to hold a patent?

    a. Abraham Lincoln

    b. Thomas Jefferson

    c. George Washington

    d. Theodore Roosevelt

9. What invention was created by Theodore Maiman?

    a. maser

    b. kevlar

    c. laser

    d. microwave oven

10. Which of the following inventions was not invented by a woman?

    a. Barbie Doll

    b. square-bottomed paper bags

    c. torpedo guidance system

    d. Corn Flakes®

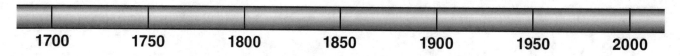

Teacher Lesson Plans for Language Arts

Biography

Objectives: Students will learn to apply their language arts skills in reading and writing biographies.

Materials: copies of Focus on a Colonial Inventor: Ben Franklin (page 46); Biographies (page 47); Selected Biographies of American Inventors (page 48); Write An Inventor's Biography (page 49); Inventor Organizer (page 50); Write Your Own Biography as an Inventor (page 51); access to biographies of inventors

Procedure

1. Reproduce and distribute the pages listed above. Have students read page 46 independently or together as a class.

2. Have students choose a biography from the list on page 48 or others of their choice and complete the discussion notes on page 47.

3. Have students complete the organizer and personal biography on pages 50 and 51. Encourage students to perceive of themselves as inventors.

Assessment: Have students complete discussion notes on page 47 and share information with their classmates. They can also share their personal biographies done on page 51.

Almanacs and Persuasive Essay

Objectives: Students will learn to apply their language arts skills in using and creating an almanac and writing persuasive essays.

Materials: copies of Using an Almanac (page 52) and Create Your Own School and Community Almanac (page 53); copies of Persuasive Essay—The Greatest Invention (page 54) and Persuasive Essay Planner (page 55); access to encyclopedias, inventor biographies, and Internet sites

Procedure

1. Reproduce and distribute the pages listed above.

2. Review instructions for using an almanac.

3. Help students begin to create a school or community almanac. Offer suggestions to get them started on the topic.

4. Lead a discussion with students about the greatest invention and review the instructions for doing the essay planner. Allow time in class to complete both drafts of the essay.

Assessment: Have students share their information from almanacs and their school or community almanacs. Encourage students to read aloud portions of their persuasive essays about the greatest invention.

Teacher Lesson Plans for Language Arts *(cont.)*

Vocabulary and Literature

Objectives: Students will expand their knowledge of words and terms associated with inventions and read fiction related to science and invention.

Materials: copies of Proverbs and Sayings (page 56); Vocabulary in Context (page 57); Einstein Anderson: Child Scientist (page 58); Einstein Anderson books by Seymour Simon

Procedure

1. Reproduce and distribute Proverbs and Sayings (page 56). Review the meaning and usage of proverbs. Encourage students to write a meaning for the listed proverbs and complete the sections on recognizing proverbs.

2. Reproduce and distribute Vocabulary in Context (page 57). Review the words with students. Have students complete the page independently. They may want to refer to selected pages in the Reading Comprehension section of this book and the Glossary (pages 94–95).

3. Reproduce and distribute Einstein Anderson: Child Scientist (page 58). Review the information and assignment with students. Help them acquire copies of this fiction series by Seymour Simon.

Assessment: Correct the activity sheets and review meanings of the proverbs and words with the class. Encourage students to share chapter information recorded on page 58.

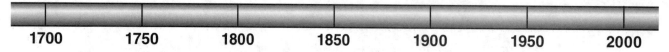

Focus on a Colonial Inventor: Ben Franklin

Benjamin Franklin is a model for the typical American inventor. From his youth, he saw needs and tried to create practical solutions. He was interested in swimming as a boy and wanted to go faster through the water. He observed the birds and other animals that swept rapidly through the water and designed his own paddles for hands and feet. He went faster, but they were uncomfortably heavy, so he sometimes used a kite in a good breeze to pull him across a river.

Ben would use a kite, of course, in his most famous experiment. He attached a long, pointed wire to a kite and a key to the kite string near his hand. During a lightning storm, he felt the electric shock from the key. Ben had proved that lightning was a form of electricity. He was fortunate the electric shock didn't kill him, but his accounts of the experiment made him famous throughout Europe, where he was honored by universities and scientific organizations. Franklin used the information from the experiment to invent the lightning rod, which protected homes and barns from lightning strikes, a major cause of fire in colonial America. He also entertained friends and important community leaders with a series of electrical experiments, including efforts to electrocute a turkey and send electric shocks through his friends.

Franklin was a very successful printer and publisher of *Poor Richard's Almanack*, an annual publication filled with advice, weather predictions, and witty sayings that amused readers. Many of his other inventions centered on business, personal, and community needs. The Franklin stove was more efficient for heating homes and cooking. He invented a stepladder stool, a rocking chair with a fan, and a device for getting books from high shelves. Later, he invented bifocal glasses to help his aging eyes read better.

Some of Franklin's inventions were community-based. He helped organize the first circulating library in America, a fire department for Philadelphia, and suggested ways to protect the community from attack, deepen rivers, dispose of garbage, and keep the streets clean. He helped start a university and studied science subjects as diverse as comets, hurricanes, the behavior of insects, and medicine. Franklin was truly a creative genius and a model for every future American inventor.

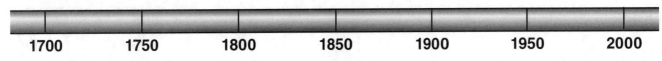

| 1700 | 1750 | 1800 | 1850 | 1900 | 1950 | 2000 |

Biographies

The biographies listed on page 48 recount the lives of famous American inventors. Some of the biographies focus on the personal lives of inventors. Others are concerned with the way the inventions were made and how they became important in American life.

Assignment

1. Read one of the suggested inventor biographies from the list on page 48 or another suggested by your teacher.

2. Complete the Discussion Notes below about your subject.

3. Use these Discussion Notes as ideas for sharing with your reading circle or class.

Discussion Notes

1. Why was this inventor important? _____

_____

2. What interesting facts did you learn about your inventor? _____

_____

3. How did the life and experiences of the inventor's youth affect his or her career as an inventor?

_____

_____

4. Name and describe three inventions or improvements on inventions that your person created.

   a. _____

   b. _____

   c. _____

5. Which of your person's ideas, designs, or inventions was the most important? Explain your choice.

_____

_____

_____

6. What was the greatest challenge your inventor faced? _____

_____

7. Are one or more of the inventions your subject created still in use today in some form or as the basis for other inventions? Where are they used? _____

_____

8. Would you have liked to have known this inventor? Explain your answer.

_____

_____

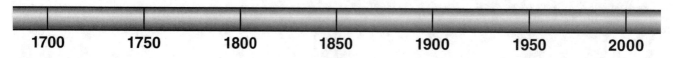

| 1700 | 1750 | 1800 | 1850 | 1900 | 1950 | 2000 |

Selected Biographies of American Inventors

Ben Franklin

Fritz, Jean. What's the Big Idea, Ben Franklin? Coward, McCann, & Geoghegan, 1976. (An amusing, easy-to-read biography of Franklin as an inventor.)

Giblin, James Cross. The Amazing Life of Benjamin Franklin. Scholastic, 2000. (A brief but comprehensive account of the life of Franklin as a creative thinker and patriotic leader.)

Harness, Cheryl. The Remarkable Benjamin Franklin. National Geographic, 2005. (A well-written and colorfully illustrated review of Franklin's career.)

Wright Brothers

Busby, Peter. First to Fly: How Wilbur and Orville Wright Invented the Airplane. Crown, 2003. (A good basic work on the life and work of the Wright brothers.)

Collins, Mary. Airborne: A Photobiography of Wilbur and Orville Wright. National Geographic, 2003. (This work issued to celebrate the 100th anniversary of the historic flight has particularly clear explanations of the Wrights' technological achievements.)

MacLeod, Elizabeth. The Wright Brothers: A Flying Start. Kids Can Press, 2002. (A well-illustrated, clever story of the great flight.)

Benjamin Banneker

Maupin, Melissa. Benjamin Banneker. The Child's World, 2000. (An easy, well-illustrated account of Banneker's life and work.)

Thomas Alva Edison

Mason, Paul. Thomas A. Edison. Raintree, 2002. (An excellent overview of the inventor's interests and career.)

Price-Groff, Claire. Thomas Alva Edison: Inventor and Entrepreneur. Watts, 2003. (A detailed account of Edison's inventions and business life.)

Williams, Brian. Thomas Alva Edison. Heinemann, 2001. (A complete overview of Edison's inventive career.)

George Washington Carver

Carey, Charles W. George Washington Carver. The Child's World, 1909. (A good introduction to Carver's life and contributions.)

MacLeod, Elizabeth. George Washington Carver: An Innovative Life. Kids Can Press, 2007. (An interesting and visual account of this inventor's life and career.)

Alexander Graham Bell

Reid, Struan. Alexander Graham Bell. Heinemann, 2001. (A complete and graphic account of Bell and his many inventions.)

Ross, Stewart. Alexander Graham Bell. Raintree, 2001. (A well-illustrated account of Bell's inventions.)

Williams, Brian. Bell and the Science of the Telephone. Barron's, 2006. (A very graphic, clear, and light account of Bell's discovery.)

Robert Fulton

Pierce, Morris A. Robert Fulton and the Development of the Steamboat. PowerPlus Books, 2003. (A very detailed and visual account of the Fulton's many interests.)

Other Biographies

Marx, Christy. Grace Hopper: The First Woman to Program the First Computer in the United States. Rosen, 2004. (An interesting account of Grace Hopper's career.)

Riddle, John and Whiting, Jim. Stephen Wozniak and the Story of Apple Computer. Mitchell Lane, 2002. (A brief, easy-to-read account of the inventor's life.)

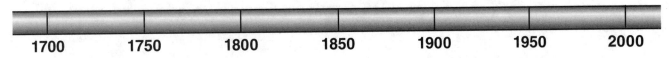

Write an Inventor's Biography

Directions: Choose one of the inventor biographies listed on page 48 or another recommended by your teacher. Use the following graphic organizer as a cluster for writing a 4-paragraph biography of your inventor. To start, complete each section in the blank organizer on page 50.

Early Life

- date
- place of birth
- schooling
- childhood interests
- personal facts about childhood and teen years
- family information

Focus on One Invention

- needs the inventor recognized
- problems to be solved
- type of invention
- costs
- uses of the invention
- success of the invention

Inventor's Name

Other Inventions and Ideas

- other invention interests
- successes and failures
- the most interesting invention
- partners, colleagues, and assistants

Personal Evaluation

- your feelings about the inventor
- importance of the inventor and his or her inventions

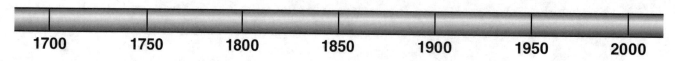

Inventor Organizer

Directions: Complete the graphic organizer below using the organizer outline from page 49 to guide your ideas. Use your findings to help you write your 4-paragraph biography on your own paper.

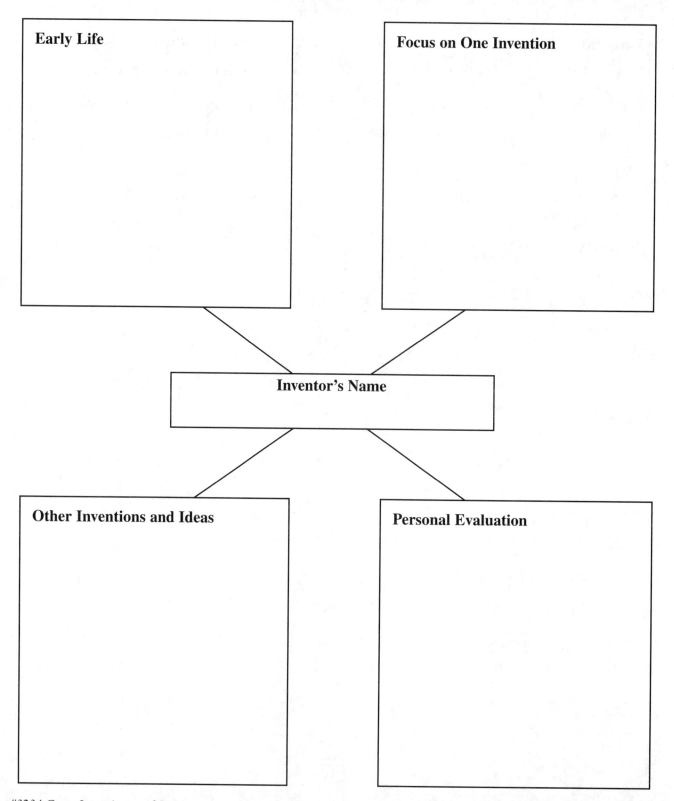

Early Life

Focus on One Invention

Inventor's Name

Other Inventions and Ideas

Personal Evaluation

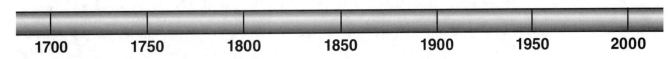

Write Your Own Biography as an Inventor

Directions: Write a three-paragraph biography of your life. Imagine that you have decided to become an inventor to meet a special need that you recognized. Describe how you approached the problem and your solution. Tell why you would like to become an inventor. Write your thoughts and ideas below, then write your final draft on your own paper.

Paragraph 1. Your Life Up to Now

_____

_____

_____

_____

_____

_____

Paragraph 2. Your Invention—The Need and Your Solution

_____

_____

_____

_____

_____

_____

Paragraph 3. Why You Would Like to Be an Inventor

_____

_____

_____

_____

_____

_____

_____

Using an Almanac

Poor Richard's Almanack was a yearly almanac published for 26 years by Benjamin Franklin starting in 1732. They were immensely popular and contained a wide variety of facts, sayings, weather predictions, astronomical information, historical dates, and many similar pieces of information.

Almanacs are still published today, and they have a wealth of information, although they usually don't have the witty sayings that were one of the popular features of Poor Richard's. Some of the topics in modern almanacs include information about cities, countries, sports, famous people of the past and present, astronomy, education, current events, science and medicine, awards, and hundreds of other subjects.

Directions: Using any almanac, find three interesting facts about each of the topics listed below.

Geography (cities, states, countries, rivers, etc.)

1. _____
2. _____
3. _____

Sports

1. _____
2. _____
3. _____

Awards/Medals/Honors

1. _____
2. _____
3. _____

Disasters (bombings, volcanic eruptions, earthquakes, etc.)

1. _____
2. _____
3. _____

Famous People of the Past or Present

1. _____
2. _____
3. _____

Current Events (events that occurred this year)

1. _____
2. _____
3. _____

Other Interesting Facts

1. _____
2. _____
3. _____

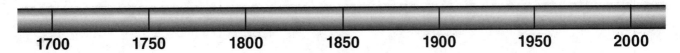

Create Your Own School and Community Almanac

Directions: List information about your community and school under the topics listed below. Be accurate and complete. Think of the almanac as a tool for new students to learn about your area.

Name and location of your community:_____

_____

Name and location of your school:_____

_____

Major rivers, lakes, oceans, or seas near your community: _____

_____

Important people in your community or school: _____

_____

Number of grades, students, teachers and families in your school:_____

_____

Number of people in your community: _____

_____

Types of jobs held by parents in your classroom and community: _____

_____

Organized sports, teams, and leagues where students play:_____

_____

Colleges in or near your community: _____

_____

Parks, recreation areas, or vacation areas near your community: _____

_____

Famous people of the past from your community and school: _____

_____

Famous events that happened in the past in your community: _____

_____

Important businesses in your community: _____

_____

Inventors, inventions, and discoveries from your community:_____

_____

Persuasive Essay—
The Greatest Invention

Directions: Write a persuasive essay about the greatest invention in American history. Choose one from the suggested list of inventions below, or choose one of your own.

Suggested American Inventions

- electric light bulb
- calculator
- cell phone
- airplane
- bifocal glasses
- basketball
- motion-picture projector

- liquid-fueled rocket
- laser
- plastic
- computer
- telephone
- Internet
- telegraph

- typewriter
- assembly line
- phonograph (record player)
- atomic bomb
- sewing machine
- electronic television
- steamboat

Organizing a Persuasive Essay

Your essay should have at least four paragraphs organized like this:

1. The opening paragraph should clearly express your opinion and indicate why the invention is important.
2. The second paragraph should describe all of the evidence you can think of to support your opinion. (This could include personal experiences, the opinions of experts, and careful reasoning.)
3. The third paragraph should describe the arguments and evidence against your position and your counterarguments and reactions to these arguments.
4. The concluding paragraph should briefly restate your position and clearly draw together all the elements of your thinking.

Pre-write

Your pre-write planning should be arranged in the order below. Use the Persuasive Essay Planner on page 55 to write your ideas for each paragraph. Write your final draft on your own paper.

1. your opinion/importance of the subject
2. supporting evidence/your experiences
3. arguments against your opinions/your counterarguments and response
4. concluding statement

Sharing Your Writing

1. Complete the first and final drafts of your persuasive essay.
2. Share your essay with a classmate.
3. Read part of your essay to the class.
4. Post your essay on the bulletin board.

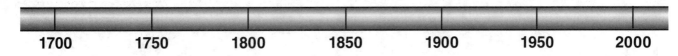

Persuasive Essay Planner

Title: _____

Paragraph 1 (your opinion/importance of the subject)

_____

_____

_____

_____

Paragraph 2 (supporting evidence/your experiences)

_____

_____

_____

_____

_____

Paragraph 3 (arguments against your opinions/your counterarguments and response)

_____

_____

_____

_____

Paragraph 4 (concluding statement)

_____

_____

_____

_____

Proverbs and Sayings

Ben Franklin was famous for the sayings that he included in *Poor Richard's Almanack*. Some of them are listed here. Read each saying and write what you think is the meaning in your own words. The first one is done for you.

1. "Three may keep a secret if two of them are dead." *Secrets are hard to keep.*

2. "Nothing is certain but death and taxes." _____

3. "God heals, and the doctor takes the fees." _____

4. "Lost time is never found again." _____

5. "Fish and visitors smell in three days." _____

6. "The greatest talkers are the least doers." _____

7. "He that lieth down with dogs shall rise up with fleas." _____

8. "A lie stands on one leg, the truth on two." _____

9. "Keep your eyes wide open before marriage, half shut afterwards." _____

10. "God helps them that help themselves." _____

11. "What you would seem to be, be really." _____

12. "No gains without pains." _____

Recognizing Proverbs

Try to complete these proverbs.

"An apple a day keeps _____"

"Early to bed, early to rise, _____"

"Practice makes _____"

Complete Your Own Proverbs

Complete these proverbs based on your own experiences with life.

"A miss is as good as a _____"

"Too many cooks _____"

"Beauty is only _____"

"He who opens a school door _____"

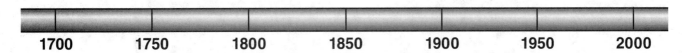
Vocabulary in Context

Directions: Complete the sentences below using the words from the word list.

Word List			
chemurgy	microchip	telegraph	patent
phonograph	filament	assembly line	diaphragm
Morse code	polio	iron lung	incandescent
transistor	laser	interchangeable parts	

1. In the 1930s and 1940s, many children contracted _____, a disease that damages or destroys lungs and cripples its victims.

2. Thomas Edison invented the _____, a device that records and reproduces sounds.

3. A _____ is a tool used to do surgery using light.

4. A _____ is a thin, flexible material that vibrates and helps produce sounds.

5. _____ is a series of "dots" and "dashes" used to send messages on a _____.

6. The invention of the _____, a series of electronic switches smaller than a pencil point, was essential to the development of many electronic inventions.

7. Henry Ford's use of the _____ to organize workers and machines made it possible for him to increase production using _____.

8. Edison's most famous invention, the _____ light bulb, used a _____ inside a bulb.

9. Nearly all inventors file for a _____, which is a government grant of sole rights to the invention for a period of time.

10. A _____ is a collection of wires and switches with more than half a million components.

11. Many children with polio had to use an _____ to help them breathe.

12. George Washington Carver was a brilliant scientist who developed _____, a science of finding new uses for plants.

Einstein Anderson: Child Scientist

The series of books listed below features an elementary-school child with a strong interest in science and invention. His nickname is "Einstein" because he is always solving problems and untangling mysteries by applying the elementary principles of science. Each book has 10 different chapters and stories featuring Einstein and his friendly rival, Margaret, who is determined to outthink him. The subjects in these books range across every kind of science including principles of light, water pressure, biology, pollution, air, electricity, zoology, radioactivity, space, and many other subjects in physics. The author, Seymour Simon, is a noted children's science author.

Assignment

1. Select one of the titles listed below. Read the book.
2. Choose any three chapters to name the problem in the story, list the science subject involved, and explain Einstein's solution to the problem. Write your ideas below.
3. Share your responses with the class.

Chapter Title: _____

The Problem:_____

_____

Science Subject: _____

Einstein's Solution: _____

_____

Chapter Title: _____

The Problem:_____

_____

Science Subject: _____

Einstein's Solution: _____

_____

Chapter Title: _____

The Problem:_____

_____

Science Subject: _____

Einstein's Solution: _____

_____

Titles by Seymour Simon

Einstein Anderson, Science Sleuth

Einstein Anderson Shocks His Friends

Einstein Anderson Sees Through the Invisible Man

Einstein Anderson Makes Up for Lost Time

Einstein Anderson Goes to Bat

*Einstein Anderson Science Detective —
The Distant Stars*

*Einstein Anderson, Science Detective —
The Tall Tale*

*Einstein Anderson, Science Detective —
The Impossible Bend*

*Einstein Anderson, Science Detective —
The Hurricane Machine*

*Einstein Anderson, Science Detective —
The Icy Question*

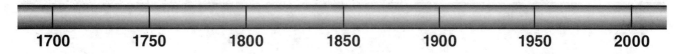

| 1700 | 1750 | 1800 | 1850 | 1900 | 1950 | 2000 |

Teacher Lesson Plans for Social Studies

Time Lines and Researching Inventions

Objectives: Students will derive information from a time line and develop research skills.

Materials: copies of Time Line of American Inventions (page 62); Time Line of American History (page 63); Researching Inventions (page 64); reference materials including books, encyclopedias, texts, atlases, almanacs, and Internet sites

Procedure

1. Collect available resources so that students have plenty of materials from which to find information.

2. Review the concept of a time line using the school year as an example. Describe and explain appropriate procedures and materials for conducting research on inventors.

3. Reproduce and distribute the Time Line of American Inventions (page 62), Time Line of American History (page 63), and Researching Inventions (page 64). Review the various events listed on the American inventions time line.

4. Instruct students to list additional dates on the time line as described in the assignment on page 63. Students may want to use the readings from the beginning of the book to help them locate the 12 extra dates for their time lines.

Assessment: Verify the accuracy of the dates and events that students added to the time line. Assess each student's ability to research inventors. Encourage oral responses and sharing of information.

Using Maps

Objective: Students will learn to use and derive information from maps.

Materials: copies of Mapping Inventions and Inventors (pages 65–66); atlases, almanacs, and other maps and invention sources for reference

Procedure

1. Review the map of the United States on page 65 and the invention facts listed on page 66. Ask students to identify a few states. Assign the map activity on page 66.

2. You may want to help students gain facility in recognizing the names of states by doing part of the activity together and then have students complete the map.

Assessment: Correct the map activity together. Check for understanding and review basic concepts as needed.

Teacher Lesson Plans for Science

Electricity Experiments

Objectives: Students will understand how to make and use an electroscope in static electricity activities and how to create and use electromagnets and telegraph equipment.

Materials: copies of Focus on Ben Franklin: Making an Electroscope (page 67); Modifying an Electroscope (page 68); Making a Telegraph Model (pages 69–70); Sending Morse Code (page 71); Using Morse Code (page 72); Electromagnets (page 73); common science materials listed on each page such as batteries, wire, balloons, foil, etc.

Procedure

1. Review the instructions for making an electroscope on page 67. Provide the necessary materials and encourage students to experiment with the device. Help students modify the electroscope using the instructions on page 68. Ask students to describe the results with each model.

2. Review the instructions on pages 69 and 70 for making a telegraph model. Provide the necessary materials and encourage students to patiently fine-tune their apparatus until the clicker works. Once students have their apparatus operational, have students use the instructions on page 71 to send and receive simple messages. Students can then practice using Morse code using page 72.

3. Review the instructions on page 73 for the procedure for creating an electromagnet. Provide materials and encourage students to develop stronger electromagnets as instructed.

Assessment: Encourage students to share their results in oral discussions after each experiment is completed.

Planes and Phones

Objectives: Students will understand how to use the principles of flight to replicate model planes and design their own. Students will learn to use the physics of sound to create and modify model telephones.

Materials: copies of Become Your Own Airplane Designer (pages 74–76); copies of Fishing Line Phones (pages 77–78); common science materials listed on pages, including fishing line, paper, cups, rulers, etc.

Procedure

1. Review the instructions on pages 74 and 75 for making each paper plane. Do one plane at a time. Demonstrate each step and refer students to the guided illustrations. Encourage students to try different modifications on their planes as they fly them indoors. Students can use these modifications and ideas for making their own planes (page 76).

2. Review the instructions on pages 77 and 78 for making fishing line phones. Provide the necessary materials and encourage students to extend the concept by sending telegraph messages over the phones and in making longer phones.

Assessment: Encourage students to share their results in an oral discussion after each experiment is completed. They could also organize their ideas and write up their results.

Teacher Lesson Plans for Science *(cont.)*

Kites and Plants

Objectives: Students will understand how to make and fly tetrahedral kites and gain insights into seed germination, phototropism, and geotropism.

Materials: copies of Tetrahedral Kites (pages 79–81); Becoming an Agricultural Scientist (page 82); Agricultural Science: Phototropism and Geotropism (page 83); Agricultural Science: Plant Nutrients (page 84); Agricultural Science: Growing Plants from Plants (page 85); science materials as listed on each page, such as straws, fishing line, seeds, etc.

Procedure

1. Review the instructions on pages 79, 80, and 81 for making and flying a tetrahedral kite. (Do an online search for tetrahedral kites to help you better understand the directions.) Use the illustration to help demonstrate how to make one cell of the kite. Encourage some students to make kites of several levels. Make sure students tie the fishing line securely and tape the paper carefully for best results.

2. Review the instructions on pages 82 through 85 for each planting activity. Encourage students to examine the growth of the plant during germination and to observe and discuss the effects of geotropism and phototropism (responses of plants to gravity and light). Help students evaluate the importance of plant nutrients and the germination of new plants from the sweet potato.

Assessment: Encourage students to share their results in an oral discussion after each experiment is completed. They should keep records to share during the plant experiments and suggest future experiments.

Making Car Models

Objectives: Students will understand how to make and test a variety of model cars from discarded materials.

Materials: copies of Make Your Own Car Model (pages 86–88); science materials as listed on the pages, such as straws of different diameters, small boxes, foam trays, bottle caps and drink lids, tape, dead batteries, etc.

Procedure

1. Review the instructions on pages 86 and 87 for making a model car from discarded materials. Use the illustrations to suggest possible car designs.

2. Demonstrate to students how to make an axle using a thinner straw inside a straw with a wider diameter.

3. Encourage students to continually modify and improve their vehicles by trying different suggestions and ideas.

4. Use page 88 to help students test their vehicles on an inclined plane such as a table with one set of legs down or a large, flat board.

Assessment: Encourage students to share their results in an oral discussion after they have completed their vehicles and tested them.

Time Line of American Inventions

1712—Sybilla Masters patents a cornmeal grinder.

1741—Ben Franklin develops the Franklin Stove.

1752—Ben Franklin performs his famous kite experiment.

1752—Franklin invents the lightning rod.

1784—Franklin invents bifocal glasses.

1794—Eli Whitney gets a patent for his cotton gin.

1798—Eli Whitney develops a factory system of rifle production using interchangeable parts.

1807—Robert Fulton's steamboat, the *Clermont*, makes a test run.

1831—Cyrus McCormick invents the mechanical reaper, which can cut, thresh, and bundle grain.

1836—Samuel Colt invents the revolver.

1837—Samuel Morse invents magnetic telegraph and Morse code.

1842—Crawford W. Long uses ether as the first anesthetic.

1844—Charles Goodyear patents the process of vulcanizing rubber.

1846—Elias Howe invents the first successful sewing machine.

1849—Walter Hunt invents the safety pin.

1861—Richard J. Gatling invents the machine gun.

1867—The typewriter is invented.

1868—Thomas Edison registers a patent for an electronic vote recorder.

1869—John Wesley Hyatt patents celluloid, the first plastic.

1873—Chester Greenwood invents earmuffs at the age of 15.

1876—Alexander Graham Bell invents the telephone.

1876—Thomas Edison creates his research center in Menlo Park.

1878—Edison invents the phonograph.

1879—Edison produces the first incandescent light bulb, electric generator, motor, and electric light system.

1893—Whitcomb Judson invents the zipper.

1901—Alexander Graham Bell invents the tetrahedral kite.

1902—Willis Carrier invents an air conditioning system.

1903—The Wright brothers make the first powered flight by a heavier-than-air machine.

1913—Henry Ford introduces the moving assembly line.

1923—Vladimir Zworykin patents the first television camera.

1924—Zworykin patents the first television picture tube to receive pictures.

1926—Robert Goddard launches the first liquid-fueled rocket.

1931—Walter Carothers invents nylon, the first artificial fabric.

1946—J.P. Eckert and J.W. Mauchly design ENIAC, the first fully electronic computer, for the U.S. Army.

1947—John Bardeen, Walter Brattain, and William Shockley invent the transistor.

1960—Theodore Maiman creates the first laser.

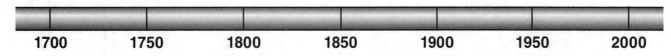

Time Line of American History

Directions: List 12 events in American history to add to the time line on page 62. These could include other inventions, wars, presidential elections, natural disasters, or sporting events. Then choose one of these events to illustrate, color, and label on a blank paper. Be sure to list all dates in chronological order.

Date   **Event in American History**

_____

_____

_____

_____

_____

_____

_____

_____

_____

Researching Inventions

Directions

1. Choose one of the inventions listed on the time line on page 62 or any other invention approved by your teacher.

2. Find out all of the information that you can about the invention, why it was created, problems the inventor had, the design of the original invention, and similar facts. Use books about inventors and inventions and approved Internet sources.

3. Make a display folder like the one in the organizer below to illustrate your presentation.

4. Present your information to a group or the entire class.

Organizing Your Information

Use the graphic outline below to organize your facts and design your display folder.

Inventor:_____

Invention: _____

The Need (what the invention was designed to fix, improve, or make possible)	**Materials** (tools and materials used to build the invention)
Problems (troubles, problems, and difficulties that the inventor encountered)	**The Idea** (the inventor's idea that solved the problem)
How It Worked (how the design or model operated)	**Importance** (why the invention is important/what it does or did)

1700   1750   1800   1850   1900   1950   2000

Mapping Inventions and Inventors

Use the United States map below with the directions on page 66.

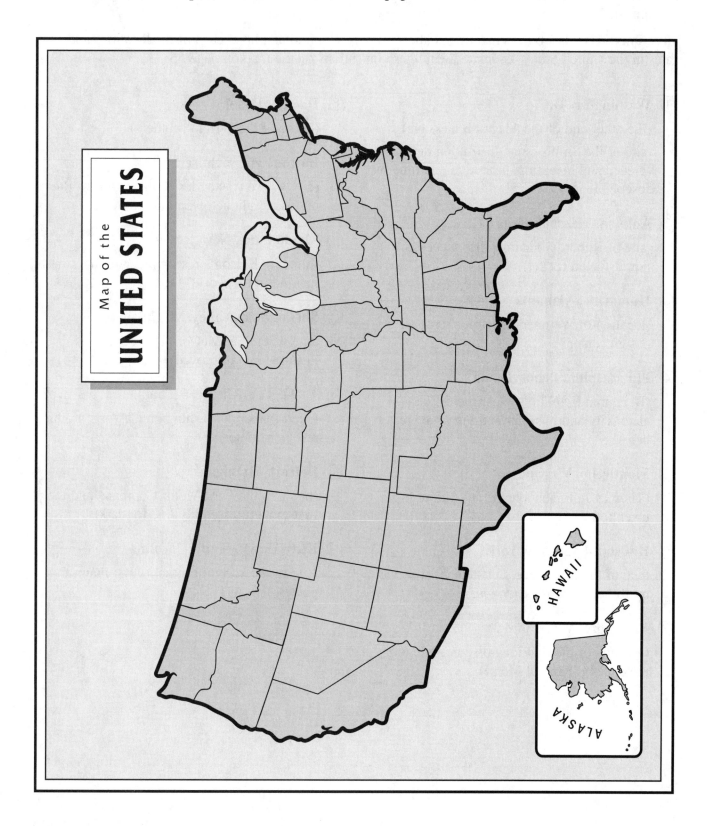

Map of the
UNITED STATES

HAWAII

ALASKA

| 1700 | 1750 | 1800 | 1850 | 1900 | 1950 | 2000 |

Mapping Inventions and Inventors *(cont.)*

Use almanacs, atlases, encyclopedias, history texts, the Internet, and other sources to help you with this assignment.

Directions: Use the sources mentioned above to help you find and label each of the localities and states in the United States associated with these inventions on the map on page 65.

① **Washington, D.C.**

(the other end of the telegraph message)

(site of the Smithsonian Institution devoted to science and invention, headed at one time by Joseph Henry)

② **Auburn, Massachusetts**

(site of Robert Goddard's first successful liquid-fueled rocket)

③ **Huntsville, Alabama**

(location of Wernher von Braun's rocket design center)

④ **Philadelphia, Pennsylvania**

(Benjamin Franklin's experiments with electricity and many inventions were created here)

⑤ **Monticello, Virginia**

(Thomas Jefferson's home and site of his inventions)

⑥ **Hudson River, New York**

(site of the first successful steamboat service by Robert Fulton's *Clermont*)

⑦ **Baltimore, Maryland**

(one end of the first long-distance telegraph message by Samuel Morse)

⑧ **Dayton, Ohio**

(home of the Wright brothers)

⑨ **Boston, Massachusetts**

(city where Alexander Graham Bell worked on his telephone invention)

⑩ **Menlo Park, New Jersey**

(home to Edison's research center, the first of its kind in the world)

⑪ **Shenandoah Valley, Virginia**

(site where the McCormick reaper was invented and improved)

⑫ **Tuskegee Institute, Alabama**

(site of George Washington Carver's product research center)

⑬ **Detroit, Michigan**

(home to the Ford Motor Company and the first modern assembly line for cars)

⑭ **Kitty Hawk, South Carolina**

(site of the Wright brothers' first manned, powered flight)

Focus on Ben Franklin: Making an Electroscope

Ben Franklin was fascinated by electricity, which in his time only existed as static electricity. Batteries and current electricity were developed in the 1800s. Franklin used a Leyden jar that could store static electricity to do parlor tricks and give electrical shocks to his friends. The electroscope (device for detecting electricity) on this page can be used to detect the presence of a static charge. When finished, modify your electroscope using the activity on page 68.

Materials

clear, plastic cups	clear tape
aluminum foil	clear, plastic wrap
bare copper wire	balloons
scissors	pushpin
Manila folder or index card	

Directions

1. Cut 8 to 10 small pieces of aluminum foil about 1 square centimeter in size or smaller.

2. Place the pieces of foil in a clear, plastic cup.

3. Fit a piece of clear, plastic wrap over the top of the cup and tape the plastic wrap in place with clear, removable tape.

4. Inflate a balloon, tie it, and rub it along your hair, sweater, or another article of clothing about 30 times. **Rub in one direction only.** This will create a static charge. (Rubbing back and forth will erase a static charge.)

5. Hold the charged balloon next to the plastic cup. The aluminum foil pieces should be drawn to the side of the cup toward the balloon.

Try This

Work with a partner. Hold two balloons next to the jar on opposite sides. What happens to the foil pieces? Can you get the foil to leap across the jar or go back and forth?

Modifying an Electroscope

Complete the activity below after you have made an electroscope from page 67.

Directions

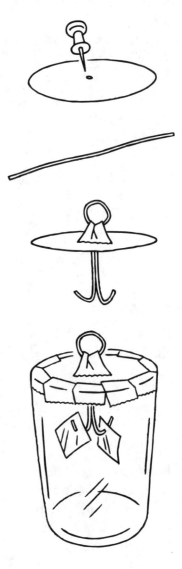

1. Take the plastic wrap off of the cup and remove the loose pieces of aluminum foil.

2. Cut a lid to fit the jar made from a Manila folder or index card.

3. Use the pushpin to make a small hole in the center of the lid you cut out.

4. Make a loop with the wire and push the pointed end of the wire through the hole so that it extends down about two inches. Use a piece of tape around the wire at the hole so that it does not slip.

5. Fold the two prongs of wire up in opposite directions.

6. Cut out two square centimeter pieces of aluminum foil. Be sure the pieces are very small and light.

7. Use the pushpin to make a hole at the top of each piece of foil. Hook one piece of foil on each wire hook. Tape the lid tightly onto the plastic cup.

Using the Electroscope

• Rub an inflated balloon along your hair, sweater, or another article of clothing about 30 times. **Rub in one direction only.** (Rubbing back and forth will erase a static charge.)

• Touch the loop of wire above the cup with the charged balloon.

• Observe the pieces of foil on the wire. They should push apart because they are both receiving the same charge. Like charges repel each other just as the same poles of a magnet repel each other.

Try This

Continue moving the charged balloon along the side and bottom of the cup. Observe what happens to the wire and the foil pieces on the wire.

_____

Did the wire appear to vibrate when the charged balloon touched the bare top of the wire or when the balloon was moved across the side of the clear cup?

_____

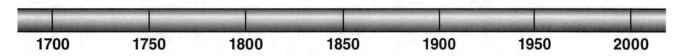
Making a Telegraph Model

The telegraph was the first of the great communications inventions. The telephone and many other inventions were based on the telegraph and the use of electromagnets.

Materials

2 long (1/2-inch) metal thumbtacks

2 feet of thin, insulated copper wire

small piece of rough sandpaper (2 in.^{2})

piece of soft wood

small hammer

2 nails with heads

scissors

battery (size C or D)

rubber bands

4 large paper clips

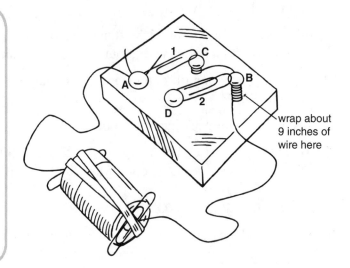

wrap about 9 inches of wire here

Part A

1. Cut a piece of thin, insulated wire about 4 inches long.

2. Strip 1 inch of insulation from each end of the wire this way:
   a. Fold the sandpaper in half.
   b. Wrap the sandpaper over one end of the wire.
   c. Squeeze, twist, and pull on the sandpaper until the insulation comes off the wire.
   d. Do the same with the other end of the wire.

3. Wrap one end of the wire around the shaft of a large metal thumbtack.

4. Wrap the small end of a large paper clip (1) tightly around the same thumbtack shaft.

5. Stick the thumbtack with the wrapped wire and paper clip into the wood at point A as shown on the illustration.

Part B

1. Wrap 2 strong rubber bands tightly around the fresh, new battery.

2. Wrap the hanging bare wire end from Part A tightly around the center of a large paper clip.

3. Insert the paper clip with the wrapped wire between the rubber band and the positive pole (top) of the battery.

4. Strip one inch of insulation off the other end of the remaining long piece of wire. Remember to squeeze, twist, and pull the insulation off.

5. Wrap this bare end of the wire around another large paper clip and slip the paper clip between the rubber band and the negative pole (bottom) of the battery.

Making a Telegraph Model *(cont.)*

Part C

1. Hammer two nails into the wood at points B and C. Be sure that the nail head at point B is about an inch above the wood.

2. Wrap the long piece of wire extending from the battery around the nail at point B. The nail will have about 9 inches of wire around it. You do not need to strip off the insulation.

3. Strip the insulation off one inch of the remaining wire at the end of point B and wrap it around the nail at point C.

4. Insert the thumbtack into the wood at point D.

5. Wrap the smaller end of a large paper clip (2) around the thumbtack (point D). Push the tack into the wood so that the large end of the paper clip is about 1 centimeter above the nail at point B.

How the Telegraph Works

A telegraph works by electromagnetism. When you push down the paper-clip switch (paperclip #1) and touch the nail at point C, you connect the battery and wire in a complete circuit. The electricity flows from the battery and through the wire that surrounds the nail at point B. The wired nail becomes an electromagnet, which pulls against the clicker, the paper clip (2) centered above the nail. When you release the paper-clip switch at point C, the electricity is stopped and the electromagnet is disconnected, letting the paper-clip clicker bounce back up.

Using the Telegraph (Fine-tuning the apparatus)

You will need to experiment with the paper-clip switch and especially the paper-clip clicker above the nail to make your machine work.

- Try moving the paper-clip clicker slightly higher if the paper clip sticks to the nail or slightly lower if it doesn't strike the nail.

- Try hooking a second paper-clip or a penny over the clicker paper clip for more weight.

- Try using a second battery next to the first one for more power. (Make sure the positive pole touches the negative pole.)

- Try using another metal piece, such as a report-folder clamp, for the clicker.

Sending Morse Code

Samuel Morse invented the code using "dots" and "dashes" to send messages across the wires. It was almost as important as the apparatus itself.

Messages are sent in Morse code using only "dots" and "dashes" combined to represent letters. You send a dot by briefly touching the telegraph. A "dash" is held a little longer. If you have created a telegraph model, use it to practice sending a message. Use these suggestions for sending your messages:

dot = 1 count	between letters = 3 counts
dash = 3 counts	between words = 7 counts
between the "dots" and "dashes" within a character = 1 count	

International Morse Code

A	B	C	D	E	F
·—	—···	—·—·	—··	·	··—·
G	H	I	J	K	L
——·	····	··	·———	—·—	·—··
M	N	O	P	Q	R
——	—·	———	·——·	——·—	·—·
S	T	U	V	W	X
···	—	··—	···—	·——	—··—
Y	Z	0	1	2	3
—·——	——··	—————	·————	··———	···——
4	5	6	7	8	9
····—	·····	—····	——···	———··	————·
Period	Comma	?	!		
·—·—·—	——··——	··——··	—·—·——		

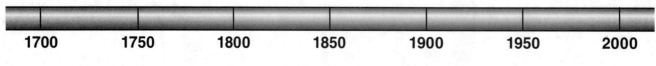
Using Morse Code

Directions: Use the Morse code shown on page 71 to convert your name and other words into code. Use these examples to help you.

cat   _•_•   •_   _ _____

friend ••_•   •_•   ••   •   _•   _•• _____

your name _____

safe _____

mother _____

help _____

rescue _____

prize _____

March 15 _____

thank you _____

4 dogs, 3 birds _____

1972 _____

Directions: Practice sending and receiving messages with a classmate. Write your own message in Morse code below and then trade with a friend. Can you figure out each other's messages?

_____

_____

_____

_____

_____

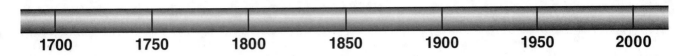
Electromagnets

The electromagnet was a critical invention in the telegraph, the telephone, and many other important devices of the 19th century. This page shows several ways to make and use an electromagnet. The essential components of an electromagnet are a current of electricity traveling though a coil of wire around a piece of metal.

Materials

2 feet of thin, insulated copper wire

2-inch square of rough sandpaper

nail or small bolt

battery (C or D)

small paper clips

small rubber band

scissors

iron filings (optional)

Making the Electromagnet

1. Use the piece of rough sandpaper to take off 1 inch of insulation at each end of the wire. Squeeze the sandpaper over the insulation, twist back and forth, and pull. It may take several times to get each end of the wire down to bare copper. (You may also use scissors to scrape the insulation off.)

2. Wrap the wire about 10 times around a nail or a bolt in neat coils. (Leave about 2 inches of wire on the end before you start wrapping the wire.)

3. Wrap a small rubber band firmly around a battery.

4. Place one bare end of the wire under the rubber band against the metal pole at the top of the battery.

5. Place the other bare end of wire under the rubber band against the metal at the bottom of the battery.

Using the Electromagnet

- Hold the tip of the nail or bolt above a few small paper clips. How many did the magnet pick up?

- Wrap the wire 10 more times around the nail or bolt. How many paper clips can you pick up now?

- Wrap as many coils as you can around the nail or bolt. How many paper clips can you pick up now?

Try This

Do the same experiment with iron filings. If you don't have any, you can often remove them from a sandbox with a magnet.

Become Your Own Airplane Designer

The Wright brothers spent much of their wintertime in the late 1800s and early 1900s designing their own planes, testing their models, and refining their ideas as they built each new flying machine. Try the paper plane design below and on page 75, and then make your own modifications on these planes and create entirely new models to fly. Paper planes fly best when the folds are symmetrical and most of the weight is in the nose of the plane. Make your folds neat and sharp.

Delta One

Materials: 8 1/2 by 11-inch paper; small paper clips; clear tape; ruler

1. Fold the top of an 8 1/2 by 11-inch piece of paper down to a point one inch from the bottom of the paper. Make a sharp fold.

2. Fold the top of the model over one more inch and make a sharp fold.

3. Fold the model in half down the middle.

4. Fold the paper up one inch from the center fold on both sides of the fold.

5. Fold one top corner of the model down 2 1/2 inches from the center fold.

6. Fold the other top corner down 2 1/2 inches from the center fold.

7. Tape the corners to the center fold.

8. Fold the wings along the same lines used in steps 4 and 5. Fold the rear wings up one inch from the tips.

9. Place one small paper clip on each side of the nose of the plane and one on the nose to hold the fold.

Flying the Model

- Hold the plane with the thumb and middle finger with the forefinger against the rear of the model.

- Launch the plane with a flick of the wrist. Do not throw too hard.

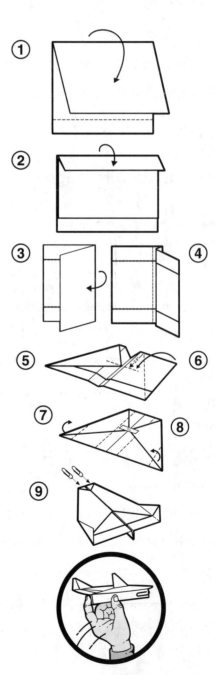

Become Your Own Airplane Designer *(cont.)*

The Swept Wing Flyer

Materials: 8 1/2 by 11-inch paper; small paper clip; ruler

1. Fold the top of an 8 1/2 by 11-inch paper 2 inches down from the top.

2. Fold the paper another 2 inches down from the top.

3. Fold the paper again 2 inches down from the top.

4. Fold the paper along the center so that the model is symmetrical.

5. Draw a line one inch from the center fold on both sides of the fold.

6. Fold up along these lines to create a fuselage.

7. Measure a half-inch in from the edges of the model (wings) and draw a line along each edge.

8. Fold up along these edges to create the rudders, or stabilizers, of the plane.

9. Place a small paper clip on the nose of the plane.

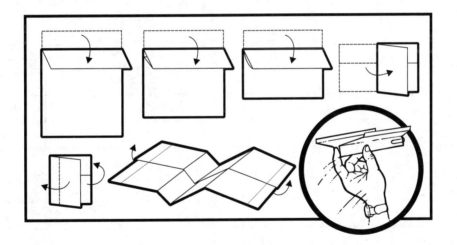

Flying Tips for Paper Planes

- Hold the plane with the thumb and middle finger and the forefinger against the rear of the model.

- Launch the plane with a flick of the wrist. Do not throw too hard.

- Adjust the number of small paper clips on the nose of the plane to get the maximum flight.

- Try the plane in different conditions, such as large indoor areas and outside in calm weather.

- Adjust the rudders up or down or one up and one down for different types of flight.

- Experiment to determine which conditions and rudder arrangement works best for distance, loops, and control of the plane.

Become Your Own Airplane Designer *(cont.)*

Design and Make Your Own Model Planes

Use the paper plane examples on the previous pages to create your own paper plane designs. Be creative. Try many different designs for wings, fuselage, and rudders. You may want to start by modifying some of the models you just built.

Tips to Remember

- The majority of the weight of the plane should be in the nose of the plane.
- Streamlined designs fly farther and better.
- The rudders should be adjusted up or down to get the best results.
- The creases should be sharply folded.

Directions: Write the steps for creating your paper plane design. Remember to be very specific so that another person can easily make the design. Then trade directions with a classmate. Try to recreate each other's paper planes. Modify your directions as needed afterwards.

1. _____

2. _____

3. _____

4. _____

5. _____

6. _____

7. _____

8. _____

9. _____

10. _____

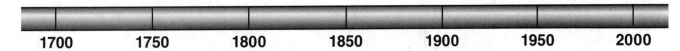

Fishing Line Phones

Alexander Graham Bell invented the first working phone when he was trying to use the new telegraph technology to create a device that would help deaf people hear. Many inventions occur accidentally, but most inventors quickly recognize the value of their unexpected creations. You can use the basic principles of the transmission of sound to create your own simple telephone. Complete the activity below and on page 78 with a partner.

Materials: roll of fishing line; large plastic cups; scissors; small paper clips; pushpins; measuring tape

Directions

1. Use a pushpin, compass point, or small nail to poke a hole in the bottom of 2 plastic cups.

2. Cut a piece of fishing line about 20 feet long (or about the width or length of the classroom).

3. Insert one end of the fishing line through the bottom of one cup and tie it securely to a small paper clip. Pull the paper clip firmly against the bottom of the cup.

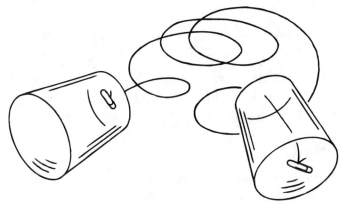

4. Insert the other end of the fishing line through the bottom of the other cup and tie it securely to another small paper clip. Pull the paper clip firmly against the bottom of the cup.

Using the Fishing Line Phone

- Students need to go outside or into a large open room and stand as far apart as the fishing line permits.

- One student places the phone over his or her ear.

- The other student talks clearly and slowly into the cup without shouting.

- The listening student should clearly hear the conversation.

Why It Works

1. The sound made by the student speaking bounces off the bottom of the cup, which serves as a diaphragm.

2. The plastic cup diaphragm vibrates and transfers these vibrations along the fishing line to the bottom of the other student's plastic cup, which acts as a diaphragm and causes the air in that cup to vibrate.

3. The vibrating air in the second cup causes the air in the student's ear to vibrate and the sound is heard.

Fishing Line Phones *(cont.)*

> ### Materials
>
> roll of fishing line   pushpins
>
> large plastic cups   Morse code (from page 71)
>
> scissors   tin cans (several sizes)
>
> small paper clips   other cups

Sending Morse Code

- Use the fishing line phone you made from page 77. Stretch it out and have both partners listen with the cup over the ear.

- Using the Morse code on page 71, one partner should tap the cup with his or her fingernail to send simple words.

- The other partner needs to "decode" the message. This partner should use a pencil and paper to write down the "dots" and "dashes." Use page 71 if needed to transfer the dots and dashes into letters.

Party Line

- Two teams with phones should stand as shown in the picture at right angles to each other.

- One partner should go to the middle and wrap the fishing line from their phone around the other line so that the four cups are connected.

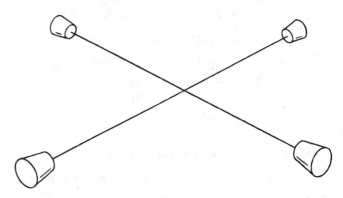

- Stretch out so that all four lines are tight.

- One person should talk while the others listen. Students should take turns talking.

How Far?

1. Replace your fishing line with a much longer piece of fishing line. Try 40, 60, or 80 feet in length.

2. Reconnect your cups and stretch out the line. Make sure the line is tight and not touching any tree, person, wall, or other object. (The vibrations are deadened when they touch any object.)

3. Test your telephone. You will probably be able to hear.

4. Try other materials such as tin soup cans or large, family-sized cans.

5. Send messages by tapping or talking.

6. Try using a pencil or metal utensil to beat out a musical pattern.

7. Keep adding fishing line to see how far the vibrations will carry.

Tetrahedral Kites

Alexander Graham Bell invented the telephone and worked on many other devices designed to help people. He was particularly fascinated by the concept of the tetrahedral shape. He designed and built the first tetrahedral kite with light balsa wood. It was strong enough to carry a 220-pound man into the air. He used a boat to pull it fast enough to get the kite and rider airborne.

> **Materials**
>
> straight straws   fishing line
>
> art tissue paper   kite string
>
> clear tape   scissors
>
> small plastic rings or plastic paper clips (no metal)

The Tetrahedral Kite

The tetrahedral kite is made from 4 cells—each of which is a tetrahedron. Each of these triangular prisms is quite strong and very good at catching the wind. It may be helpful to do an online search for tetrahedral kite directions. That way, you can use colorful photographs to help guide you through the process. Be sure to remind students not to use any metal materials in their kites.

Making the Tetrahedral Cell

1. Thread fishing line through 3 straws and tie them to make the triangular base of the cell.

2. Thread fishing line through 2 more straws and tie it firmly to 2 sides of the triangular base so that one side of the cell is now upright.

3. Thread fishing line through 1 more straw and tie it firmly to the upright side and the base so that a triangular prism or tetrahedron is now formed. Make sure all of the fishing line knots are tight.

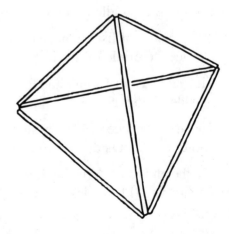

4. Do not cut off any extra fishing line. Leave a few inches of fishing line for connecting the cells.

5. Make 3 more tetrahedral cells in exactly the same way.

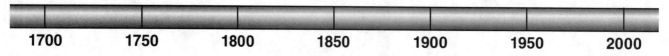
Tetrahedral Kites *(cont.)*

Assembling the Tetrahedral Kite

1. Arrange 3 tetrahedral cells on the bottom and 1 cell on top as shown in the illustration. (They leave a triangle in the middle on the base.)

2. Use extra pieces of fishing line to firmly connect each of the bottom cells and to connect the top cell to each of the bottom cells.

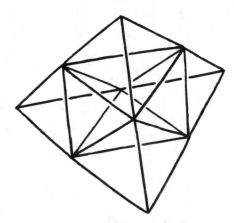

Covering the Tetrahedral Kite

1. Use art tissue paper (about 6 inches by 12 inches or a little larger) to cover 2 upright faces of the tetrahedron.

2. Fold the paper over the 2 faces and use clear tape to tape the paper to the frame and to overlap the paper so that the faces are clearly covered.

3. Use the same procedure to cover the same 2 faces of each tetrahedron.

4. All the covered faces must face in the same direction.

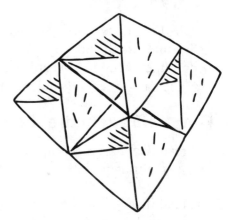

Making a Bridle

- The kite will fly without a bridle, but in some wind conditions, a bridle is helpful for stability.

- Cut 2 pieces of fishing line about 1 foot long to make a two-legged bridle for the kite.

- Tie one piece of fishing line to the bottom corner of an outside bottom cell.

- Tie another piece of fishing line to the other bottom corner of the outside bottom cell.

- Tie the end of each fishing line to a small plastic towing ring (like a plastic ring or plastic paper clip —no metal).

- Let the fishing line dangle away from the paper-covered spine of the kite.

- Tie a kite string to the plastic ring and have the string on a reel for letting out the line.

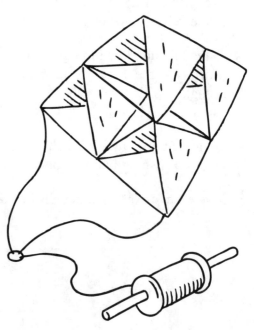

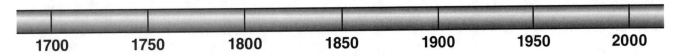
Tetrahedral Kites *(cont.)*

Flying the Kite

1. You can use the bridle or just tie a round plastic piece to the top of the kite.

2. Tie kite string securely to the plastic piece.

3. Wait until there is a fairly strong and steady breeze to fly this kind of kite.

4. Take the kite to a playground, open field, or park well away from power lines, trees, and buildings.

5. Face the kite into the wind, then gradually let out a little line.

6. Pull the kite with the line until the wind catches and lifts the kite.

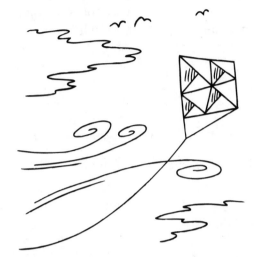

7. You may also throw the kite into the air or let a friend throw it up.

8. Let out the line as the breeze lifts the kite higher into the air. Let the wind take the kite as high and far as it can go.

Making a Bigger and Better Tetrahedral Kite

When Alexander Graham Bell invented this kite, he made one with many layers. You can make a bigger and better version by adding cells to your existing kite.

The 10-Cell Model

1. Make 6 more tetrahedral cells the way you made the first ones and cover them with tissue paper as you did the first ones.

2. Arrange the 6 cells facing the same direction with triangular spaces between each cell.

3. Use 4-inch pieces of fishing line or fishing line dangling from each cell to connect the cells to each other.

4. Arrange the 4-cell model directly on top of the 6 cells so that a larger tetrahedron is formed.

5. Use 4-inch pieces of fishing line or fishing line dangling from the cells to connect each of the six cells to the tetrahedral kite.

Flying the 10-Cell Model

This model is heavier but more stable in flight and less likely to twirl around in the wind. It stays aloft longer and doesn't usually need a bridle.

Try This — Making a 4-Layer (20-cell) Kite

Add another layer of 10 more cells to make a 4-layer kite. Connect them in the same way making a tetrahedron with all the open faces in the same direction. You can keep adding layers to make even larger kites.

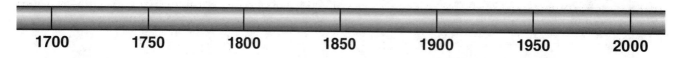
Becoming an Agricultural Scientist

George Washington Carver made enormous contributions to the improvement of agriculture because of his invention of new uses for food plants and his understanding that some plants, such as beans, returned nutrients to the soil while others, like corn, took large amounts of nutrients from the soil in order to grow. You can observe the actual process of development in the activity below and on page 83.

Materials

lima bean seeds   self-sealing (gallon size) plastic bags

pinto or shell bean seeds   white paper towels

corn seeds   magnifying glasses

pumpkin seeds

Directions

1. Soak 2 pieces of white paper towels in water, making them completely wet.

2. Spread the paper towels in the bottom of a large, clear plastic bag.

3. Carefully place 5 lima bean seeds in a line along the soaking paper towels.

4. Place 5 pinto, shell, or other small bean seeds next to the line of lima bean seeds.

5. On the other side of the paper towels, place 5 corn seeds and 5 pumpkin seeds.

6. Do not seal the bag. Place the bag with others in a tray in a lighted part of the room or outside during the day. (You can string a long piece of fishing line across the room and use clothespins to hook the bags onto the line.)

Examining Germination

- Examine your seeds daily. Use a magnifying glass to observe the swelling of the seeds, the growth of the root, and the sprouting of the stem.

- Record your observations on this chart and draw sketches of your observations.

Observation Chart

Day 1 _____

_____

Day 2 _____

_____

Day 3 _____

_____

Day 4 _____

_____

Sketches

Agricultural Science: Phototropism and Geotropism

Complete the activity below after you have completed the activity on page 82.

Directions

1. Add an ounce or two of water to keep your paper towels and seeds moist, but do not cover them.

2. Examine the roots and notice that they are growing down.

3. Examine the stems and notice that they are growing up.

4. Seal the bag, then carefully turn it over so that the roots are facing up and the stems are facing down.

5. Place the bags upside down in their containers or shelf, or hang them upside down from the fishing line.

6. Observe them every other day for a week. Record what happened to the roots, the stems, and the seeds. Draw sketches with each observation.

> ### Materials
> seed bags from page 82
>
> magnifying glasses
>
> small water cups (2 or 3 oz.)

Observation Chart

1st Observation _____

_____

2nd Observation _____

_____

3rd Observation_____

_____

Sketches

Geotropism and Phototropism

- Geotropism is a response to gravity in which roots grow downward.

- Phototropism is a response to light in which stems grow toward the light.

Try This

- Make sure your seeds are still damp and switch the direction of the bags once more.

- Observe the reactions of the plants and describe what happened. _____

_____

_____

- Why do you think some of the plants are dying? _____

_____

Agricultural Science: Plant Nutrients

Complete this activity with a partner.

Directions

1. Cover a foam tray with 3 layers of paper towels.

2. Spread a few grass seeds on one part of the tray.

3. Spread birdseed (which has many types of seeds) on another part of the tray.

4. Use a spray bottle with water to dampen the towel, but don't drench it.

5. Spread a half-inch layer of potting soil on another tray.

6. Spread a few grass seeds on one part of the soil.

7. Spread birdseed on another part of the soil.

8. Use the spray bottle to dampen the soil, but don't drench it.

9. Label each tray so that you remember which type of seeds is where. Set both trays in a lighted area of the room.

> ### Materials
> flat foam trays   potting soil
>
> grass seeds   birdseeds
>
> white paper towels   spray bottle with water

Observing Results

Observe the growing pattern for each tray.

- Which tray of seeds sprouted first?
- Which types of seeds sprouted first?

Examine the new sprouts. Describe some of them and draw sketches.

Descriptions

Sample 1 _____

_____

Sample 2 _____

_____

Sample 3 _____

_____

Sample 4 _____

_____

Sketches

Which tray of plants stopped growing? _____

Which tray of plants had many plants still growing? _____

Potting soil has many nutrients that are necessary for plant growth. How did the seeds grow in the tray with potting soil? _____

_____

Agricultural Science: Growing Plants from Plants

George Washington Carver was famous for his work with sweet potatoes. These experiments will allow you to observe potato growth. Complete this activity with a partner.

Materials

potatoes	sweet potatoes
plastic cups	toothpicks
plastic or metal dinner knife	potting soil
paper towels	spray bottle

Growing Potatoes

1. Examine the potato carefully. Count the number of dents (called eyes) in the potato. The new potato plants will sprout from these eyes.

2. Use a plastic or metal dinner knife to cut the potato into several pieces. Make sure that each piece has at least one or two eyes.

3. Plant the potato pieces in cups and cover them with potting soil or a paper towel.

4. Spray water on the soil or paper until it is damp but not soaked.

Observations

Examine the potatoes every few days. Look for sprouts and roots. Describe the potatoes' changes.

_____

_____

_____

Try This

Use toothpicks to hold a sweet potato in a cup above the bottom of the cup. Fill the bottom of the cup with wet paper towels or water so that it is touching part of the potato.

Observations

Some of the sweet potatoes will start to sprout at the top or sides of the potato. If too much water is used, the potato will rot. Describe what happened to your sweet potato.

_____

_____

_____

Make Your Own Car Model

Henry Ford and other early American carmakers designed their own vehicles based on the technology of the day. The influence of the bicycle was evident in most early cars and many refinements were added as roads improved and more customers bought cars. You can design your own model car from throw-away materials found around the house. Use the ramp described on page 88 to test the speed and sturdiness of your design.

Suggested Materials

thin straws	jumbo straws
foam tray	small plastic lids
wood barbecue skewers	old batteries or penny rolls
heavy tag board	scissors
small check box or food take-out box	straight pins
yardstick or broomstick	tape

Making Your Vehicle

1. Study the vehicle samples illustrated below.

2. Choose one model to make using the suggested materials listed above or others of your choosing.

3. Do not try to be exact in your design.

4. Use the suggestions below and on page 87 for making the wheels turn and increasing speed and momentum.

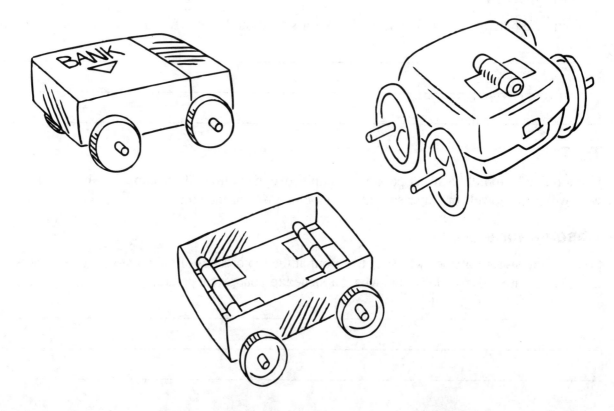

Make Your Own Car Model *(cont.)*

Creating the Body and Frame

1. Use a small check box, foam tray, food take-out box, or other small box for the body of the vehicle. You want the body to be light but sturdy.

2. Decide which end will be the front of the vehicle.

Smooth Speedy Wheels and Axles

1. Make a smooth, speedy axle by placing a long, thinner straw inside a short, wider straw.

2. Tape the short, wider straw to the bottom of the box or tray frame near one end of the frame.

3. Thread the thinner straw through the wider one.

4. Stick each end of the thinner straw through a bottle top, a coffee or soda lid, or any sturdy round objects you can use for wheels.

5. Make sure the thinner straw with the wheels turns easily inside the larger straw.

6. Attach a second set of wheels and axle to the other end of the box or tray.

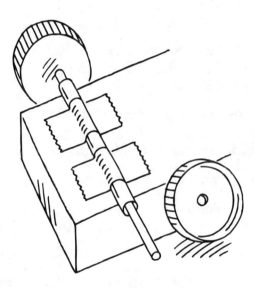

Better Wheels

Try these suggestions to make the wheels faster and stronger:

- Insert one thin plastic lid inside another and tape them together.

- Cut a piece of tag board the same size as each wheel and tape the circular piece inside each lid.

- Face two lids next to each other and tape them together.

- Place two lids back to back and tape them together.

- Split the ends of the straw axle that extend beyond the lids and tape these ends securely to the outside of the wheel or use straight pins in the straw axle on each side of the wheel to keep the wheel from bending.

- Improve the speed and durability of your vehicle by replacing the straw axles with wooden skewers or round pencils. You could also slip these or similar materials into the straws to reinforce the straw axle.

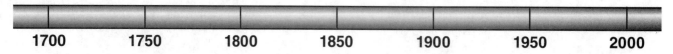
Make Your Own Car Model *(cont.)*

Testing Your Vehicle

1. Use a portable school table with legs that fold down when not in use, or a wide board propped onto a desk or chair.

2. Adjust the table firmly so that one set of legs is folded up and the other legs are folded down.

3. Tape a yardstick or broomstick as a divider down the middle of the table so that you can test two cars at the same time or race against a classmate.

4. There should be a flat runway on the level ground at the end of the board or table.

5. Test your model on the slanted table several times. Determine what improvements you can make on the model.

6. Try the modifications described below.

Modifying Your Vehicle

Try these suggestions for improving your model:

- Replace the rear wheels on your model car with larger wheels such yogurt lids, soft drink lids, or even larger wheels cut from thick, stiff materials.

- Reinforce these new wheels the way you did the smaller wheels and attach them to the axle.

- Test this model on the runway. Determine if the larger wheels increase the car's speed. You can compare the speeds by timing the run, noticing if one car went farther than the other, or racing your car with and without the big wheels against another car.

- Try another set of big wheels on the front of the car. Determine if the speed is improved.

Increasing Momentum

Momentum describes the driving force of a moving object. You may increase the speed of your car by positioning a weight on certain areas of the vehicle.

- Tape a battery or a roll of pennies somewhere on the rear of the car. Test the car on the runway. Compare the speed using another car, timing it, or counting until the car stops.

- Try locating the weight in different areas of the car, such as the rear, the front, the center, under the car, or elevated above the body of the car.

- Compare your results. Try a second battery or penny roll.

| 1700 | 1750 | 1800 | 1850 | 1900 | 1950 | 2000 |

Create Your Own Invention

So You Want to Be an Inventor!

People of all ages and backgrounds have become inventors. What makes inventors unique is that they see a problem or sense a need and try to create a tool, a machine, a system, or a device to meet that need or solve the problem. Inventors haven't always had educational opportunities, but they have all shown qualities of persistence, determination, and creative problem solving. Use these activities to help you become an inventor today.

Looking for Ideas

- Look around your classroom, on the playground, in your house, and throughout your neighborhood for ideas. Ask your parents, neighbors, coaches, and older siblings what type of invention they wish they had. Listen to even the silliest suggestion—it might lead you to a serious need or plant an idea in your mind that you can use.

- Think about common household chores, toys, closets, pet care, and food preparation.

- Check sports equipment connected with baseball, basketball, football, skateboards, tennis, swimming, and bicycles. (One inventive baseball player created a better catcher's mask to protect the throat.)

- Let your mind roam through lots of ideas from the impossible to the silly to the serious.

Inventive Children

Study some of these inventions attempted by children:

- a machine that pitches tennis balls for practice
- an automatic plant-watering device
- a combination cap and nose warmer
- a combination hat and glove holder (to prevent losing them)
- a snow saver (for the hot summer)

- an elevator for cats
- a rodent elevator for hamsters and mice in cages
- an automatic feeder for rabbits and Guinea pigs
- a better exercise machine for pet mice
- a handwriting copy machine for making two copies of written homework at a time

Brainstorming

List several ideas for inventions that you have considered and which might be possible to make using easy-to-access materials.

_____

_____

_____

_____

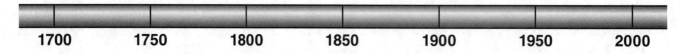

Create Your Own Invention *(cont.)*

Creating the Invention

1. Choose your invention topic from the choices you listed on page 89. Make sure it is reasonable and can be done.

2. List the tools and materials you will need and the help you need from an adult.

3. Draw a sketch of the invention as you see it in your mind. Label the parts and materials.

Invention Name: _____

What the Invention Does:_____

_____

Tools and Materials: _____

_____

_____

Adult Help Needed: _____

_____

_____

Sketch of Proposed Invention:

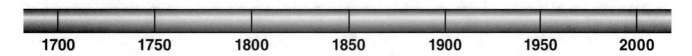
Create Your Own Invention *(cont.)*

Making the Invention

List the step-by-step procedure you intend to use to make your invention. Write these instructions clearly enough so that others can understand and follow your directions. Then construct your invention after you have gathered all of the materials.

Step 1: _____

_____

Step 2: _____

_____

Step 3: _____

_____

Step 4: _____

_____

Step 5: _____

_____

Step 6: _____

_____

Step 7: _____

_____

Field Testing and Refining Your Invention

Test your invention. Look for what works and what is not working well. Refine your invention by checking each component or part of the device. Keep looking for ways to make it work better by substituting materials or adjusting the apparatus.

The Invention Convention

Demonstrate your invention for the class and the teacher at an "invention convention" with all the classroom inventors. Describe your problems and your solutions. Explain how you might still improve your model.

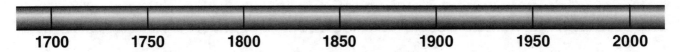

Create Your Own Invention *(cont.)*

Advertising Your Invention

In the space below, sketch your ideas for an advertisement for your invention. Be sure to include the following elements: name of invention, what the invention does, picture of invention, why people should buy it, and the price for the invention. Create your final advertisement on a separate sheet of blank paper. Be sure to make it colorful and eye-catching.

Annotated Bibliography

Nonfiction Middle Grade Picture Books

St. George, Judith and Small David. <u>So You Want To Be An Inventor?</u> Philomel, 2002. (Caldecott-winning collaborators have created an amusing and colorful introduction to some American inventors.)

Williams, Marcia. <u>Hooray For Inventors</u>. Candlewick, 2005. (This book includes colorful and amusing anecdotes of many inventions in history.)

Collective Biographies

Hegedus, Alannah and Rainey, Kaitlin. <u>Bleeps and Blips to Rocket Ships: Great Innovations in Communications</u>. Tundra, 2001. (An interesting series of vignettes about communications breakthroughs in North America from photography to fiber optics.)

Jefferis, David. <u>Flight: Fliers and Flying Machines</u>. Franklin Watts, 1991. (A superbly illustrated time line account of flying machines from the earliest days to the present.)

Vare, Ethlie Ann and Ptacek, Greg. <u>Patently Female: From AZT to TV Dinners, Stories of Women Inventors and Their Breakthrough Ideas</u>. Wiley, 2002. (This book includes brief accounts of women inventors.)

The Invention Process

Dowswell, Paul. <u>Great Inventions: Medicine</u>. Heinemann, 2002. (A good survey of medical innovations and inventions.)

Dyson, James. <u>A History of Great Inventions</u>. Carroll & Graf, 2001. (An excellent overview of inventions and how they occurred.)

Haven, Kendall. <u>100 Greatest Science Inventions of All Time</u>. Libraries Unlimited, 2006. (This book includes brief and informative accounts of the most essential inventions in human history.)

Markham, Lois. <u>Inventions That Changed Modern Life</u>. Raintree, 1994. (A good survey of the main inventive trends of the last two centuries.)

Platt, Richard. <u>Eureka! Great Inventions and How They Happened</u>. Kingfisher, 2003. (This book includes interesting, brief accounts of many modern inventions.)

Platt, Richard. <u>Inventions Explained: A Beginner's Guide to Technological Breakthroughs</u>. Holt, 1997. (A clear, colorful overview of invention from prehistory to the present.)

Rossi, Ann. <u>Bright Ideas: The Age of Invention in America 1870–1910</u>. National Geographic, 2005. (A well-integrated account of the effect of innovation on the American people in the late 1800s and first part of the 20th century.)

Samuel, Charlie. <u>Inventors and Inventions in Colonial America</u>. PowerKids Press, 2003. (This book includes easy but interesting accounts of several Colonial inventors.)

Tomacek, Stephen M. <u>What A Great Idea: Inventions That Changed The World</u>. Scholastic, 2003. (This book includes brief accounts of fundamental human inventions.)

Turvey, Peter. <u>Timelines Inventions: Inventors & Ingenious Ideas</u>. Watts, 1992. (This book includes graphic, colorful accounts of modern inventions.)

Wyatt, Valerie. <u>Inventions</u>. Kids Can Press, 2003. (A good child-centered book devoted to inventive ideas in modern life.)

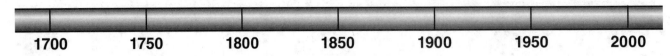

| 1700 | 1750 | 1800 | 1850 | 1900 | 1950 | 2000 |

Glossary

agriculture

the science of raising crops and animals for food

alternating current

electrical current that rapidly changes direction

anesthetic

a drug used to reduce pain during surgery

antibiotics

medicines designed to kill infections

arthroscopic surgery

a procedure using a small camera and tools to operate inside joints and body organs

assembly line

a line of workers and/or machines used to make a product in steps

aviation

flight

chemurgy

the science of finding new uses for plants

circuit

a complete path (such as one taken by an electric current)

combine

a machine that harvests grain

cotton gin

a device used to separate cotton fibers from seeds

current

flow (of electricity, etc.)

diaphragm

thin, flexible material that vibrates

dumbwaiter

a small elevator used to carry items between floors

dynamo

a generator for making electricity

electromagnet

a magnet created by running an electric current through a coil of wire

fertilizer

any substance which puts nutrients into the soil

fiber optics

a method of sending light signals at high speed through glass or plastic tubes

filament

a thin thread of material used in light bulbs

glider

a light aircraft without an engine that flies on air currents

hybrid

a plant developed by humans by mixing other plants

hydrofoil

a boat that travels on top of the water

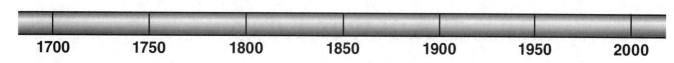

| 1700 | 1750 | 1800 | 1850 | 1900 | 1950 | 2000 |

Glossary *(cont.)*

incandescent

hot enough to glow

ingenious

clever and creative in solving problems

interchangeable parts

machine-made parts that are exactly alike and can be replaced easily

iron lung

a device invented to help polio victims breathe

laboratory

a place where experiments are done

laser

a device using amplified light as a tool in surgery, reading CDs, and in fiber-optics

MRI scanner

a device used to see inside soft tissue

microchip

a collection of wires and switches with over half a million components

Morse code

series of "dots" and "dashes" used to send messages on the telegraph

patent

a government grant to an inventor giving him sole rights to the invention for a period of time

phonograph

a device that records and reproduces sounds

polio

a deadly contagious disease that crippled children and damaged their lungs

propeller

a center rod with attached paddles used to provide lift and forward movement in a plane, boat, etc.

rudder

a structure at the tail of a plane, boat, etc., used to make horizontal changes in course

Smithsonian Institution

an institute in Washington, D.C. built to encourage science and learning

survey

to measure (land, etc.)

telegraph

a machine that sends messages coded with "dots" and "dashes"

transistor

electronic switches smaller than a pencil point

vacuum

a space without air

vibrations

fast movements up or down or from side to side

wing-warping

the Wright brothers' system of changing wing shapes to control lift

Answer Key

Page 36
1. b
2. d
3. a
4. d
5. b
6. a
7. d
8. d
9. b
10. a

Page 37
1. a
2. d
3. c
4. b
5. d
6. c
7. a
8. c
9. d
10. d

Page 38
1. a
2. a
3. a
4. b
5. c
6. d
7. b
8. a
9. b
10. a

Page 39
1. b
2. a
3. c
4. c
5. d
6. b
7. b
8. a
9. d
10. a

Page 40
1. b
2. d
3. b
4. b
5. a
6. c
7. b
8. a
9. b
10. b

Page 41
1. d
2. b
3. c
4. b
5. c
6. a
7. b
8. d
9. d
10. c

Page 42
1. a
2. b
3. b
4. b
5. b
6. c
7. d
8. b
9. b
10. c

Page 43
1. b
2. a
3. b
4. d
5. b
6. b
7. d
8. a
9. c
10. d

Page 56
Suggested answers:
1. Secrets are hard to keep.
2. Life is mostly uncertain.
3. God is the real healer.
4. Don't waste time.
5. Don't overstay your welcome.
6. Do things instead of talking about them.
7. It matters who your friends are.
8. Lies are usually easy to detect.
9. Be choosy in whom you marry, but don't expect your spouse to be perfect.
10. Be responsible for yourself.
11. Be honest about who you are.
12. All success requires work and effort.

"An apple a day keeps the doctor away."

"Early to bed, early to rise, makes a man healthy, wealthy, and wise."

"Practice makes perfect."

Page 57
1. polio
2. phonograph
3. laser
4. diaphragm
5. Morse code; telegraph
6. transistor
7. assembly line; interchangeable parts
8. incandescent; filament
9. patent
10. microchip
11. iron lung
12. chemurgy